When I'm 64

Dr Donna Gibbs is a leading Australian educator whose publications are held in libraries and educational institutions around the world. She writes on topics as diverse as Elizabethan love poetry, children's literature, film and cyberculture. An Honorary Associate of the Australian Centre for Educational Studies at Macquarie University, Donna is currently researching the background for her new children's book, *Pocket of Secrets*.

When I'm 64

THE NEW RETIREMENT

DONNA GIBBS

NEW
SOUTH

A New South book

Published by
University of New South Wales Press Ltd
University of New South Wales
Sydney NSW 2052
AUSTRALIA
www.unswpress.com.au

National Library of Australia
Cataloguing-in-Publication entry
Author: Gibbs, Donna.
Title: When I'm 64: the new retirement/Donna Gibbs
Publisher: Sydney: University of New South Wales Press, 2008.
ISBN: 978 1 921410 20 8 (pbk.)
Subjects: Retirement.
    Retirement – Planning
    Phased retirement.
    Early retirement.
    Retirement – Psychological aspects
    Adjustment (Psychology)
Also Titled: When I'm sixty four: the new retirement
Dewey Number: 646.79

Design Di Quick
Illustrations Bill Wood
Cover photo Peter Beavis/Gettyimages
Printer Ligare

Contents

Acknowledgments

Let me begin by thanking all those people who have allowed me to interview them and so have helped to create this book. Your generous, willing responses to my questions, and the kind way in which you have supported my endeavours to explore the subject of retirement, are very much appreciated. I have such happy memories of meeting and corresponding with each of you.

Phillipa McGuinness, my editor at the UNSW Press, believed in the project from the start and has been helpful, warm hearted and wise in her assistance to me. My grateful thanks to her, to the staff of the Press and to my agent, Sheila Drummond.

My friends have been their usual tower of strength – asking after my progress, thinking of people for me to interview, finding articles for me to read, suggesting title after title only to have me brutally discard them (the titles, that is), and allowing me to jot down their every thought about retirement, without complaint. Special thanks to those who have gone the extra mile in additional ways: Deirdre

Bair, Margaret Beale, Mary Cunnane, Lori Dietrich, Bill La Ganza, Ichiro Kobayasha, Yon Maley, Diana Olsberg, Kerry-Ann O'Sullivan and Annemieke Vimal du Monteil.

In the medieval morality play, *Everyman*, the character called Knowledge utters the famous words:

> *Everyman, I will go with thee, and be thy guide*
> *In thy most need to go by thy side*

During the writing of this book, my family and friends have provided companionship such as this. My heartfelt thanks go to them here for their loving care and encouragement.

For Tony, my other self,
and in memory of
Juliet M, Mark D and Rhonda M

Preface

Tomorrow, to fresh woods and pastures new

'Lycidas', John Milton, 1638

Some time ago I ran into a retired friend at a dinner party in Sydney, Australia. Retirement was something I was contemplating seriously just then. I'd begun to think about the changes it would make to my life and how best I could prepare for it. When I saw my friend looking wonderful and relaxed across the dinner table from me, I launched into what, in retrospect, I realise was my first 'interview' for this book.

'How are you finding retirement? What are you doing?' I asked with real interest expecting an enthusiastic reply. 'It's terrible, really. I thought it would be much better', my friend replied. 'No one asks me to do anything I want to do, everyone asks me to do things I don't want to do, and I'm not sure what I do want to do. I am still adjusting to it and it is four years ago now that I have left work!' I was shocked.

Still adjusting four years later! This was an elegant, attractive, talented woman with a happy marriage, children and grandchildren, who had been admired and respected in the workplace. What had gone wrong?

Over the next few years I often talked to people about what they were doing in retirement, the thoughts and feelings they had about their experiences. I was surprised at how largely it loomed in people's lives and found that almost everyone had something to say about it. I began to understand why Hugh Mackay, the well-known Australian social commentator, defines retirement as 'one of the greatest life changes of all'.

Then I, too, was 'Unemployed at last!' and experiencing the same joyous feelings as the character who first immortalised these words in the opening sentence of Joseph Furphy's Australian novel, *Such is Life*, in 1903.

In 2006 I set off to the United States for a three-month house exchange in Connecticut with my husband, who was giving talks in different US cities about a biography he'd just completed. Sitting in the kitchen of our temporary New England home and chatting with an American writer friend who had kindly taken us under her wing, I found myself telling her I was thinking of writing a book about retirement – not a financial guide, or a chronicle of what can go wrong with health, as these aspects are well documented, but what people who are retired think, feel and do. 'That book needs to be done', she said to me.

I began serious interviewing, mostly in person, but sometimes by phone and email, while I was in the United States and Canada. As I talked to people about the subject I realised contemporary societies are dealing with unprecedented change – an explosion in the numbers of retired people who are facing 20 to 30 years of life without the structures and restrictions of work. I wondered how people used this time. Are they at a loss as to what to do with it? Do they simply fill in the time, or use it to find different kinds of meaning and fulfilment? What are the issues that concern them most and how are they dealing with them? Are these problems the same across different cultures? Such questions needed answers.

Upon my return to Australia, quite some time elapsed before I continued with my interviews. That 'elapsed' time is part of the story of being retired and I will come back to it a little later. But for the most part it was the dinner party conversation and the kitchen chat with my American writer friend that were the spurs that started me on the path which ultimately led to this book.

Getting started

Once home I found myself 'properly' retired. I thought it would be a breeze to get started on my writing and other plans, but instead I found myself doing a lot of agonising about using time productively and finding a rhythm to things. A professor from Trinity College, Dublin, had told me that his colleague, an Irish poet, had thought and talked endlessly about 'getting the rhythm' right when he retired. I found he'd hit the nail on the head. As any good poet would!

Events (a wedding in our garden; a sixtieth birthday party for a friend; serving as a juror on a rather long trial) kept intruding and gobbling up time alarmingly, though pleasantly except for the jury duty. I did begin to work on writing books for children as I'd planned to do, but I was doing this in dribs and drabs while feeling I should get my entire study/household/world reorganised first. Was this anxious muddling in and out of projects and extensive worrying what retirement would turn out to be?

My friend, Margot, told me I should give myself permission to let things take their course for about a year. She saw adjusting to retirement as coming to terms with ambiguous boundaries – finding out how much money you can or can't spend, or how much time to devote to family and friends, or to following your own pursuits, for example. She consoled me that it would all become clearer over time.

Fear of reproducing my old work routine and dithering about how to spend my time delayed my getting started on this book. But my interest in exploring people's feelings and ideas about retirement – something so intimately connected with how they define themselves and see the world – wouldn't go away. Eventually, nudged by enquiries as to how the book was going from various friends, I found myself getting started again. I set up some more interviews and was soon engrossed and working at a rhythm with which I felt comfortable. Looking back I see that the early stages of retirement are a bit like jetlag – but it takes much longer to recover.

Down to the nitty gritty

Given that the nature of retirement is changing so rapidly I wanted to keep my definition of the term fairly loose. In general, I think of retirement as leaving the regularly paid workforce. Many people semi-retire and others leave the workforce and begin another full-or part-time career, yet some of these people continue to think of themselves as retired. I chose not to exclude these people as their reactions have their own validity. But my focus is mainly on those who think they are stepping away from working as the main way of earning their living.

My method for selecting people to interview was largely through word of mouth or through a 'snowballing' technique. To begin with I interviewed friends and colleagues, and they often recommended people they knew who had retired. I visited some organisations that included retirees in their membership, and invited people from there to be interviewed.

The interviews were carried out 'live' by phone, in people's homes (lasting sometimes three hours or more when we really got involved), or in coffee shops or cafes. I also relied a lot on email to send questions and to confirm answers. Often all three methods (interviews by phone, in person and by email) were used with the same person. In fact, most of the interviews turned into longish conversations held over time. As some of the information included in the book is very personal, I have made minor changes to an individual's details where necessary, and also I have used pseudonyms throughout, except when aspects of the stories I am telling are in the public domain. In these cases, real names are used with permission.

I interviewed well over 100 people from Australia, and from other countries including the United States, Canada, France, Japan, Malaysia, The Netherlands and the United Kingdom. I also had numerous conversations about the subject of retirement with people wherever I met them. Those interviewed ranged up to 99, and there was a good gender balance. Many lived with a partner, some were widowed or lived alone by choice, some were newly retired and others had been retired for 30 years or more. I sometimes interviewed both partners from a marriage, but at other times just one partner, sometimes the wife, sometimes the husband.

Those interviewed included academics, accountants, actors, administrators, artists, athletes, authors, builders, bus drivers, business executives, butchers, chemists, cleaners, cooks, counsellors, doctors, drivers (taxi; car hire), engineers, farmers, fitters and turners, gardeners, health and aged care professionals, lawyers, librarians, machinists, mechanics, members of parliament, milliners, missionaries, insurance workers, interior decorators, nurses, office workers, plumbers, psychologists, publishers, researchers, retailers, sales people, secretaries, social workers, solicitors, teachers, technicians and telemarketers; and there were people from small and large businesses, from government institutions (including the army) and from the corporate world. There was a mix of those who had retired once, more than once, and of those who had been retired against their will, and there were variations as to how much part-time work (if any) was undertaken after retirement.

Listening to people talk about their personal experiences of retirement reveals what it is like in its different phases and in its varying dimensions. In the following pages you get to hear about it from the horses' mouths, so to speak. These days retirement is no longer seen as a last chance to put up your feet. And what is possible for men and women in the retirement phase of their lives will continue to change dramatically. New models for retirement are emerging; new possibilities beckoning. Rather than retirement being perceived as a 'one-way street', it is now viewed more, even if unconsciously at times, as a new 'career' – one you can gradually design and shape for yourself.

I found many common threads in what people had to say during our interviews. But it was the individuality of the responses offered and the honesty of many of the reflections people so willingly offered that I found compelling. The subject gave me a way of tapping into deep personal concerns, into what really matters to people at this stage of their lives, without my feeling that I was being too intrusive. The questions often led people to talk about the meaning life holds for them and to describe how retirement gives them an opportunity to know themselves better and to explore and face up to what they most value and care about. I am most grateful for the conversations I had, and hope to continue to have. They are at the heart of this book.

In the chapters that follow we hear the inside story about many different aspects of retirement – people's expectations of it; what the experience is like in the early years and further down the track; and the impact retirement has on relationships or when living alone, among other things. There is much to be learned from listening to what others have to say on these subjects, and towards the end of the book I attempt to draw together what I have learned from the perspectives offered and from my own fledgling experience as a retired person.

But for now let's look at how retirement has changed over time and what the 'new' retirement means for people in the twenty-first century.

When I'm 64

How things have changed

He had on some green Y fronty things
which I would have thought were a bit
young for someone who's retired.

'Nights in the Gardens of Spain',
Talking Heads, Alan Bennett, 1998

A visit to Madame Tussaud's waxworks provides dramatic evidence that human beings used to be much shorter than they are now. In the Baker Street branch in London, for example, you are met by diminutive, dainty replicas of the nineteenth-century authors, Charlotte, Emily and Anne Brontë, who at around five feet (152 centimetres) tall look disconcertingly like miniatures rather than actual size adults. Emily was even considered tall in the mid-nineteenth century – now she would have to have an extra 10 inches (25 centimetres) or so in height to be regarded that way.

Many societies are witnessing something similar with the ageing process. People of baby boomer age are beginning to notice that their grandparents in photos at age 65 often look a good 10 years older than people of the equivalent age today. Advances in medical knowledge, improved health care, the less physically demanding nature of work, and other factors, are resulting in a human race that is not only taller and stronger, but is living longer and looking younger. Life expectancy increased in Western countries during the 1900s more dramatically than at any other time in recorded human history, and has almost doubled since the time of the Brontës.

These changes have brought about a major shift in ideas about the nature of retirement. What it means to be retired obviously varies according to when you were born and the culture in which you live. If you are living at this point in history almost anywhere in the modern world you can be pretty sure that your retirement is going to be very different from the way others have lived out their retirement in the past.

Patterns of change

The idea of compulsory retirement was introduced during the industrial revolution when employers wanted to find a legitimate way of removing those workers who were too old or debilitated to be of use to them. Schemes of retirement at age 65 with accompanying state pensions, such as that introduced in the 1880s by the German Chancellor, Otto von Bismarck, provided a way for this to happen. Capitalism had its seamy side then as it does now. Unfortunately, many people didn't make it to pension age and if they did their pensions didn't have to last very long. Retirement was seen as the end of the road, a time when you were on the outer, and no longer of 'real' significance – a view that still has a powerful grip in the consciousness of many today.

The system of compulsory retirement often had distressing consequences, especially for men who were the breadwinners and who had invested their whole lives in their work. In the mid-twentieth century, stories of men dying soon after retirement for no obvious medical reason were not uncommon. A UK study of ageing in the 1940s attributes the deaths of healthy men after retirement to their being deprived of occupation and usefulness. Carl T, whom I interviewed about his own semi-retirement, recalls that in the 1960s when he was 19 and working for the personnel section of the Department of Civil Aviation in Victoria, Australia, he was often asked to locate the records of recently retired men who had suddenly died. He added wryly: 'It became something of a joke in the workplace that retiring was not such a good idea!'

In the early twenty-first century many countries have removed the compulsory age for retirement and raised the age that people become eligible for the pension. By 1996 all Australian states except Tasmania, for example, had followed this path, and by 2014 they will have phased in a system to bring pension eligibility for females into line with that of males, at age 65. Several countries – including Australia, the United States, Britain, Germany and

Denmark – are considering a further gradual increase in the eligible pension age (Iceland and Norway have already raised it to 67), with possible plans to link pension age with changes in longevity.

Part of the reason that governments are choosing to remove compulsory retirement and raise the pension age is because retired people are beginning to constitute a much larger proportion of the population, a trend set to increase even more rapidly in the near future. In 2025 it is conservatively estimated that people over 65 will make up at least a quarter of the population in countries such as Japan, Switzerland, Sweden, Denmark, Germany and The Netherlands, up from 18 per cent in 2005. Many other countries – including Australia, England and the United States – predict that a fifth or more of their populations will be over 65 in 2025, up from around 13 per cent in 2005.

Governments around the world are concerned to find ways to anticipate and deal with the consequences. This 'time bomb', as it is sometimes described, means ways have to be found to cater for future increases in medical, pension and general welfare costs as the ageing population expands. Japan, for example, has introduced a long-term care insurance scheme where people over 40 contribute an average of $45 a month funds to be used for care of the elderly, though it is not at all certain that this will prove adequate. Difficulties are compounded by the pattern of falling birth rates, which means fewer people will be paying taxes and there will be less money in the coffers to cover these expenses.

The arrival of baby boomers at retirement age has added a new dimension to the patterns of change. Boom time came with the sudden increase in the birth rate in many countries after World War 2, and lasted for almost two decades (1946 to 1964). The depressed living conditions of the previous generation were superseded by an economic upsurge enabling improved lifestyles and better educational opportunities. These baby boomers are beginning to exit the workforce now, or will be doing so anytime soon. Predictions that they will change what it means to be retired are widespread. A nationwide sample survey by Merrill Lynch in the United States in 2006 confirmed the company's earlier findings that baby boomers will fundamentally reinvent retirement. They claim that 76 per cent of boomers have no intention of following a 'traditional' retirement; rather, their ideal will be to cycle in and out of work, and possibly to pursue a new career in later life, a pattern already evident in the lives of many of those I interviewed for this book. As baby boomers advance further into this space they may well bring changes to retirement that have not yet touched our imaginations.

In the 1930s during the recession, and then again a few decades ago when there was high youth unemployment, early retirement was in favour in many countries; now for a variety of economic and demographic reasons, workers are being encouraged to put off retirement, or to work part-time. Christine O, who retired in 1998 from a career as a government social worker in Canberra, ACT, then later as a caterer, cooking school owner and consultant in locations around New South Wales, explains how alterations to government policies make an impact on your choices in relation to employment in the post-retirement phase:

> Things have certainly changed now because of the new superannuation laws for retirees [for example, up until the age of 74, Australians can contribute to superannuation as long as they work for 40 hours in a 30-day period]. The government believes we oldies are not on the scrap heap and are still capable of working, albeit in a part-time capacity. Now I feel pressured again to do something, but only to meet the work test. I make sure I can do other things as well.

The situation for people who have retired or are about to retire in the future is volatile. It is difficult to know how to be prepared, as the marching song of the scouts would advise! With such a heady mix of change in the air and the prospect of further technological change it seems likely that retirement will continue to morph into something new and different.

What's in a name?

The language a society uses about a subject normally evolves in response to changing attitudes towards that subject. Yet in the case of things connected with retirement and ageing, language seems to lag behind new perceptions and changing sensitivities. Amy H remarked during an interview that: 'The word "retirement" makes me feel as if I'm my mother!' And

Adrian D explained his distaste for the term: 'There is a sense of the grim reaper hanging around the word'.

Those who have largely invested their identities in work often avoid the word 'retired' to describe their post-work state, as it seems to label them as lacking occupation and/or status. Those who pass so called middle age are labelled with terms that often have a quick turnover rate. I remember when 'wrinklies' had its heyday, though thankfully that was very short lived. People try to find linguistic solutions to problems of this kind, but they often prove elusive, miss the boat, or create new problems altogether. It seems to me that in time words like 'retirement', meaning to leave the paid workforce, and its associated term 'retirees', may disappear, as they'll no longer apply with any accuracy to the stage of life they describe.

The word 'retire' comes from the French 'retirer' and has a history of usage in English going back to the 1500s. Its first recorded meaning 'to withdraw to or into a place (or way of life) for the sake of seclusion or shelter or security' is rare and other related meanings now have greater currency. In the nineteenth century when employers began to use retirement as a way to pension off aged workers, the word took on more negative connotations.

Vestiges of this attitude linger powerfully, and the expression 'to be pensioned off', still in use today, carries with it a sense of veiled criticism – though of whom or what is not necessarily clear. Interestingly, some languages such as Italian (*andare in pensione*), German (*pensionieren*) and Dutch (*met pensioen gaan*) include the idea of receiving a pension in the expression that is used for 'retire', though these languages also use alternative terms that are less fiscally oriented. The connection between being paid and being of value continues to shape much of our current thinking about life after work.

Languages other than English that also currently use words with connotations of moving away, withdrawing or retreating for 'retire' include German (*'sich zuruchziehen'*, meaning to withdraw or back away from) and French (*'prendre sa retraite'*, meaning to retreat or to withdraw into oneself). The Japanese expression *'teinen taisyoku'* (定年退職), meaning to withdraw from an occupation at a specified age, places the emphasis on the age you leave the workforce. These terms all carry a hint of the idea that once you are not actively employed in the community you are losing some of your value. The Chinese expression for 'retire' (退休) means to withdraw to rest, and it is less focused on age and more descriptive about the nature of what is to happen during the time to come. In Spanish the words *'pension por retiro'* mean 'retirement pension', but the word *'jubilación'* is also used for the word 'retirement' in many Spanish-speaking countries. In these regions, retirees have the joyous and celebratory name, *'los jubilados'* – the jubilant ones, befitting of a country that loves to dance.

The earliest usage in English of the verb 'retire', as close in meaning to the sense of leaving the paid workforce, is in the seventeenth century. The *Oxford English Dictionary* includes an extract of an entry on 30 August 1667 from the famous *Diary* of the English parliamentarian, Samuel

Pepys, who records that: 'he [Sir W. Coventry] did not think any man fit to serve a Prince that did not know how to retire and live a country life'. He is referring to a political rumour that the chancellor, whom Sir William Coventry is 'high against', is about to lose office. The meaning of 'retire' in this context is given as 'to withdraw from office; to give up one's position or occupation to enjoy more leisure'.

Finding words in English, as in any language, to describe 'retired' people, 'retirement' homes, and all things to do with being retired, such as ageing, has its difficulties. As I was writing I felt an aversion to the word 'retirees', for example, and tried hard not to include it even though the alternatives were sometimes clumsy. When the label is applied to you, as an individual, you feel depersonalised and stereotyped, as though you are identified as being past your use-by date. The term is almost always applied by others who want to lump you into a group such as superannuation funds and governments. It is not one you like to use about yourself.

I used to visit my elderly relatives in 'old people's homes' in the 1950s and 1960s, but now these places are referred to as 'retirement villages', 'retirement complexes' or by combinations of words with euphemistic uplifting connotations (for example, 'prime', 'living', 'lifetime', 'care' 'resort', 'haven', 'manor' and 'mansions'). Individual complexes are often given names that include words such as 'sunrise', 'tranquil', 'waters', and 'sylvan', suggesting a relaxed, back to nature lifestyle. It should be a comforting practice, but somehow it seems more like a sleight of hand attempt to disguise some lurking truths.

When I see these names in advertisements or on buildings I can't help but think of Evelyn Waugh's *The Loved One*, a dark, satirical attack on the Californian funeral industry, published in 1948. In Waugh's novel, 'bodies' and 'cadavers' are literally and metaphorically transformed into 'Waiting Ones' and 'Loved Ones' under the aegis of Mr Joyboy, senior mortician at the funeral parlour, 'Whispering Glades', near neighbour of 'The Happier Hunting Ground', the pet crematorium. While such a parallel is farfetched it does underline the fact that appearing to offer solace and comfort to the vulnerable can be horribly entangled with reaping commercial gain.

Choosing a suitable term to describe the elderly isn't a new concern – in the seventeenth and eighteenth centuries, for example, the word 'green' was used to describe the early part of old age. The terms currently in use generally attempt to be politically correct or introduce a touch of humour, though in many instances they seem to reinforce the idea of a cover-up. Words like 'senior citizen', 'grey power' and 'grey nomad' are examples. Terms such as 'younger-older age group' and 'third agers' (as opposed to fourth agers who have reached the pointy end of life) are alternatives with some currency, though probably little staying power. 'Elder', a person of standing and influence in a community, is the only term I can think of in this context that conveys respect and admiration.

In the early twenty-first century the word 'seniors' is in vogue. Yet the April 2007 issue of *50 Something*, the monthly magazine of the national seniors in Australia, suggests the organisation should consider a name change. The term 'national seniors' is seen as a barrier for the 50–65 year olds who don't identify with being a senior or who tend to associate the name with 'stereotypical views of activities for the elderly'. Until 2002 in the United States, *Modern Maturity* was the name given to AARP's magazine (originally the American Association of Retired Persons, but now simply AARP). It then changed its name to *AARP, The Magazine*. Perhaps the choice of an utterly bland title is a strong selling point with this age group as this magazine claims to have the largest circulation of any in the world.

Images of retirement

While the language people use to talk about the retired state is still in its Dark Age phase, visual representations of retired people have undergone a revolution. Images of such people found in the media only 10 or so years ago were those of well-behaved, neatly dressed maiden aunties and bachelor uncles – asexual, passive, kindly looking and ready to disappear quietly like the fluff on a dandelion if you were to blow softly. Today the upmarket images that accompany advertisements for the over-55 brigade are more likely to be those of well-dressed people exuding energy and a spirit of adventure, bearing expressions of perpetual ecstasy, and looking as if they are on their way to somewhere exciting.

Promotional information about retirement housing, insurance, superannuation and so on is commonly accompanied by pictures of people of mature age not just smiling, but laughing, sometimes in quite painful looking ways. The 'models' stretch their mouths wide open (and usually their arms as well), displaying all their teeth, even sometimes tipping their heads back to reveal inside the roofs of their mouths. They are hell bent on proving that they are happier than happy, that retirement is pleasure laden.

. Advertisers love to link retirement with images of happy, laughing, grey-haired very-much-in-love couples wandering along the beach in perfect weather. Alternatively, they might go for the extended family image, where grandchildren are smilingly attached to an active looking grandparent, while visiting them in their new home that clearly caters for everyone's interests ranging from fishing to photography. Mum or dad smiles her or his approval in the background.

To appeal to singles, an alternative image becoming more familiar is that of a group of retired men and women having a whale of a time, toasting the air, barely unable to refrain from jumping for joy, and sometimes doing just that. Everything is airbrushed in these images – the people, the sentiments, the surroundings. The falseness does not pass unnoticed and many people complained to me about the irritation caused by advertising of this kind.

Another trend is for humour to be used in advertisements about retirement products – jokes about turning the tables on the kids or 'the dreaded R-word', for example. And some advertisements are directed to the baby boomers themselves, specifically acknowledging them as those who will redefine retirement. The accompanying images are of active looking hikers, or maybe explorers, or else smartly dressed bikies ready to rev off on their expensive bikes. My superannuation report arrived with a picture of an elderly woman dressed in goggles and a helmet, with her gloved hands stretched forward and holding the handlebars of a motorbike that looks very much like a Harley-Davidson. The words 'Afford to dream' are stamped across the top of her head. In many of these advertisements people are advised to explore, to live life to the full, to discover a new way of life – desirable ambitions, but somehow hollow when they are claimed so exclusively and so relentlessly for this particular age group.

It feels rather mean spirited to knock this kind of advertising. Mental images of life in a hammock are rather attractive when you are getting up to join the traffic every morning and struggling to meet deadlines and please bosses. And if you are thinking of downsizing or moving elsewhere after you retire, images of a life of leisure in perpetual summer surroundings may beckon. Yet we all know these images, part of the landscape of our minds when we think about retirement, present unrealistic versions of how we will spend our lives after we leave paid employment.

New directions

Societies that value work in monetary terms generally define retirement as a time when an individual ceases to be a paid member of the workforce. This view of retirement implies an 'ending', rather than a beginning, and has a stranglehold that perhaps may never quite disappear. Even so, an alternative view of retirement as something to be celebrated, even envied, a time when you are finally free to do your own thing, also exists and is gaining ground. This is not a new way of thinking about retirement – it has always been trotted out in farewell speeches, a kind of gloss that is applied hoping there is truth in it – but now it has more substance, a firmer basis in reality.

Questions about what people will do with their 'gift' of time are of increasing interest now that there is such a longish span of life to look forward to in retirement. It may be that there will be a shift away from seeing life as divided into segments of pre- and post-retirement, and life will be viewed more as a continuum where people do different kinds of things at different stages. In some ways this is a version of the ways people like the Inuits or Aboriginal peoples, before the arrival of Europeans, viewed life. They didn't have a concept of paid work and so had no concept of retirement. Life for them was seen as a continuum without a watershed passage to 'retirement'. Whether or not modern societies adopt an attitude of this kind, it is certain that new models and new ways of thinking about age and retirement are evolving. It may be, to adapt Gerard Manley Hopkins' words, that in time retirement will 'gather to a greatness' and take on a life of its own.

The prospect of retirement

As to that leisure evening of life, I must say that I do not want it. I can conceive of no contentment of which toil is not to be the immediate parent.

Anthony Trollope

In the last year or two before retiring I thought about retirement issues almost every day. I wondered if this was how most people reacted or whether I was unusual. After all, the fact that I am going to the lengths of writing a book about the subject suggests I may not be typical. It is hard to tell what goes on in people's minds about this subject in the years leading up to retirement. Do people often think about the prospect? What do they imagine it will be like for them, and what do they think they'll do in that long stretch of time? What motivates them to take the plunge? I decided to include a group of people who were not yet retired in my interviews so I could find out.

I soon discovered different personalities deal with

retirement in extraordinarily varied ways: some slam into it, some creep up to it slowly, some think about it haphazardly from time to time, some act impulsively, some plan meticulously, and others avoid all thought of it.

Those who find the prospect of retirement enticing are sometimes prepared to move mountains to get there at the earliest possible moment. Kim P, an egg farmer who works in Kuala Lumpur, is working all hours so he can retire at 50. He wants to devote his time to flying, paragliding and scuba diving, and is already taking lessons. He dreams of having his own plane ('a spitfire would be best'), though realises this is probably out of the question.

'Is flying something you've grown interested in as you've got older?' I asked Kim. 'No', he replied. 'As a young boy I wanted to be a pilot and if not that then a policeman. My mother insisted these were very dangerous occupations. I worked on my father's egg farm instead, and now I run it by myself. But I aim to retire in five years and then I'll fly.'

Flying, not unexpectedly given its associations with freedom and escape, features quite often in people's dreams of retirement. Flying with a slightly different twist is the dream of Howard R and his wife, Dana. Howard has his own consulting business that involves his visiting locations all over New South Wales, and he recently purchased a build-it-yourself helicopter from the United States. When his helicopter is finally airborne he plans to use it to get to rural and distant areas. But when he sells his business and retires, he won't sell the helicopter. He and Dana will travel around Australia to wherever their whims take them.

Retirement is not yet a prospect for Sacha S, a financier in a Swiss merchant bank based in Sydney, but it is a regular feature of his fantasy life. He says he thinks about retirement 'all the time', even though he quite likes his job and has recently been promoted to a high level in his organisation:

> To me it represents freedom from constraints, and from
> obligations. Bliss! My life is dominated by the work routine.
> It will be a welcome change not to have that any more. I
> plan to organise my life around my hobbies – playing music,
> motorbike riding, surfing, things like that.

It sounds as though Sacha would empathise with the sentiments of the infamous Irish pool player, Danny McGoorty: 'To me a job is an invasion of privacy'.

Sometimes people think they want nothing to do with retirement and then fall under its spell unexpectedly. They find it enticing after all. Carol D, an academic in the field of education and a strong union activist, always thought she would keep working until well past retirement age – then came her 'epiphany' as she calls it. She had been unhappy for many years in her marriage and suddenly realised she had to move on. She says the decisions to retire and to leave her husband were inextricably linked.

She feels liberated at the prospect, and realises she doesn't want to waste any more time in a workplace that she is finding less and less meaningful. In her enthusiasm to begin her new life she moved forward the proposed date of exiting the workforce and now would be leaving just a matter of weeks after our interview. 'Retirement is going to be my new career', she said happily as she contemplated the possibilities ahead. I met up with Carol about six months later and asked if retirement was living up to her expectations. 'Absolutely!' she replied. 'It's like a new job, the best I've ever had. I've liked all my jobs, but in this one it's as if the boss lets me do whatever I like.'

Anthony Trollope, the esteemed Victorian novelist abhorred the idea of retirement. He was a prodigiously hard worker, famous for his 'double shifts' – rising early and writing a given number of words by 11 a.m., then going off to a day's work at the post office where, among his other accomplishments, he introduced the idea of the famous British red pillar mailbox. Right up until his death in 1882 he was well known for his habit of carrying on with his writing wherever he was – on a train, in a restaurant and so on. There are others like Trollope who choose never to retire – writers, musicians, actors, even politicians, come to mind. 'I can't imagine life without work', is a sentiment you often hear.

There are many who dislike the prospect of retirement. 'Retirement's not in my book', Stuart M, a real estate agent said to me after asking what I was writing about. And as Betty Driver who in her 86th year is playing 'Hot Pot' Betty in *Coronation Street* on ITV in the United Kingdom says: 'I don't understand these people who say they look forward to the day they retire…. I was barely getting started when I reached 60 and have no plans to retire now!'

Greg C, an actor in Canada, doesn't plan to retire either, and says actors never do. To demonstrate he told me in actor-like fashion, 'doing' all the voices, a story about his friend's elderly father. When this man turned 96 he asked his son for help with his income tax. His son gathered his father's documents together and gave them to his accountant. 'What's this?' the accountant exclaimed. 'This man has been working in his 96th year. He has income recorded!' The man's father was an actor and still appearing on the stage though in very small parts.

Doctors and dentists are another group who often choose to put off thinking about retirement for as long as possible. Simone K, a social worker attached to a hospital in Hamden, Connecticut, told me she had been talking to a doctor aged 94 doing his rounds that very morning. Graham K, a GP in Perth, chose to semi-retire some years ago at 60: 'I don't have the worry of "blow-ins" as we call them, who include drug addicts and the like. I spent about 40 years of my life dealing with the hard stuff and must say I now enjoy just seeing the patients I know. I hope to keep going as long as I can keep up to date and my health holds.'

Whether or not people think of retirement as an attractive prospect, there are many who choose to delay the possibility. The main stumbling blocks people mentioned as causing them to put off the decision include not yet having enough money to live on at that time; anxiety as to how they will fill in the time; the thought of losing the companionship of the workplace, particularly after bereavement or when you live alone; fear that pressures to provide care for others will take up all of your time; and, if partners are involved, differences of opinion as to where you will live or what you will both be doing.

Many I talked to about retirement plans said they knew precisely how many more years they'd need to continue working to be in a financial position enabling them to retire, usually a time that little bit further off than they'd like it to be. A less commonly mentioned financial stumbling block was that described by Steve F, who has his own investment company in Sydney.

The real issue in his case, he says, is worrying about providing an income in retirement that will cover the costs of his continuing to pay insurance premiums against potential claims from past projects in which he's been involved, a very costly enterprise that can involve amounts running into six figures. Steve points out that self-employed people in a range of fields, including physicians and orthodontists, are driven by many similar concerns. 'My thoughts about retirement are 98 per cent related to income issues, so that thinking about what I might actually do has a low priority'.

I asked Steve what kind of difference winning the lottery might make and was surprised to find he'd given that a lot of thought. In the kind of business he's in 'windfall projects' occur very occasionally, so thinking about the possibility isn't as farfetched as it might be otherwise. Steve knew exactly what he'd do. He'd set up a trust fund and use the money to provide hospitals with the new equipment they needed. He'd visit hospitals, talk to the doctors, research their needs, work out a business plan, and make it happen. Would he be like Nigella Lawson and leave nothing to the children, I asked? 'Sort of', he answered, 'because the best thing you can give a child is a secure job that pays well and has a purpose. The trust fund would create this possibility by allowing salaries for my daughters that wouldn't affect the capital, so the work of the trust could go on.'

Another burning ambition of Steve's that emerged during our morning coffee meeting was to fight what he sees as government corruption, though, as he puts it, he hasn't yet thought of the best way to 'light the fuse': 'An ideal retirement profile would be to work with bodies to stop public service theft of funds, get a referendum to disband state governments and to make toll ways illegal. And I'd like to organise groups of retired people, a kind of "Silverpower", to do useful things such as give half a day to act as a think tank for the police, or other organisations.'

I found it striking that Steve has a deeply embedded assumption that retirement will be a time when he will still be working. Yes, he'd like to have more time off to play competition tennis, golf, or whatever, but he imagines himself at work though in different ways, and carrying on with life in the only way he imagines possible for him.

Putting off retirement because you can't think what you will do is another common deterrent. Helen D, now in her seventies, is about to retire from a government job in Los Angeles, but is not looking forward to doing so: 'I'm not a good candidate to be interviewed as I am dreading retirement. I'm tired of working, but don't know what I will do with myself.' Mack B, who among other things used to write an unusual kind of wine column for a weekly paper says that 'What will I do if I retire?' is the real question. He doesn't yet have an answer, so he doesn't feel able to make the decision. 'I need to find something significantly different to do in retirement before I go down that path. Until I do I'll drift along doing what I'm doing', he explains.

Gemma A says 'I'm terrified of retirement'. She has frail elderly parents living in South Africa, a daughter living in Colorado, United States, and another daughter living in Melbourne.

> I know I'll be needed everywhere and I'll be torn. My parents need me to visit them regularly. I'll want to be with the kids when they have their babies. My husband's business is here [Gemma works with him at present, though she is keen to return to a career of her own] and he'll want me to be with him. I'll want to do all of these things, but I'd like to have the time and continuity needed to do something for myself as well. But I can't see that happening.

The companionship of colleagues and students has been an important factor in Kevin P's decision not to retire. A Jesuit priest for many years, he has worked in various places in the world, including Ireland, the United Kingdom and Zimbabwe. After leaving the priesthood he became an academic and is now employed at a university in Sydney. Kevin is recently married with one son from his previous marriage. He lost his other teenage son to leukaemia, a devastating experience. He says he plans to retire in 2008, around the time he turns 76, but is reluctant to do so as he knows he'll miss helping his students and the happy connections he's had with them over the years. 'Only yesterday', he said 'a Chinese student appointed me the unofficial grandfather of her new baby. It's things like that I'll miss. I've never wanted to retire. I've watched people who do – one friend, a hotshot accountant, came very close to a nervous breakdown after giving up work. You are still part of the world, but it can be a living death.'

I asked Kevin what he thought he would do in his retirement. 'I've had a long time to think about it', he smiled. 'You need a purpose, you need a reason for keeping in touch with humanity. I'll offer my services as a teacher of English in local communities, or in any other capacity where I can be useful. Or I might go to China to teach for six months.'

Our interview was held during lunch at Kevin's staff club and we'd reached the coffee stage when he recalled the words of a Jesuit who had visited his novitiate shortly after he'd entered the priesthood. Kevin suddenly saw their relevance to his present situation:

We were struggling to come to terms with the changes in our lives, and this man helped us by explaining that when we entered the novitiate we'd found ourselves looking backwards to the lives we'd left behind. But now we had to learn to turn ourselves around to look forward to a new way of life. This is how I think I will try to approach retirement.

It was one of those moments that occur occasionally in interviews when a thought or an idea suddenly creates a special kind of silence.

On the whole, then, it seems that some people think about retirement obsessively for up to a decade or more before they leave their working lives behind. Some actively choose never to retire, others dread it, put it off, or hope it will never happen. Some go through the motions of retiring but stay in denial, picking up work here and there, and remaining in working mode. Others think about it now and then over the years, and then in a more concentrated way for a year or two before actually making their exit.

Imagining...

Many people who choose to retire imagine themselves spending their time in particular ways. They think they can make a pretty good guess as to how they'll feel and what they will or won't be doing. Kay N, who is soon to retire from a 20-year career with the US Department of State presents an engaging view of how she hopes her retirement will unfold:

> I think that my life will become more like a patchwork quilt with time for study, time for volunteer activities, time for friends and family, and time for me (gym, reading, etc.).

I also imagine that I will be able to handle all the chores, such as grocery shopping and laundry, on weekdays and have the weekends for family and friends.

A Sydney psychotherapist who has not yet retired, Eleanor A, thinks she'll be busy in all sorts of different ways, but that the 'busy' you feel in retirement will be different from the busy you feel at work. There will be less pressure to meet deadlines and many of the tasks you will do are those you set yourself:

It will be like living in the weekend. That is when you feel time is yours to enjoy yourself, but also a time to catch up on tasks you've put off, or need to get done. In fact, what happens at the weekend is that you often don't complete half of what you plan. So you put some things off to the next weekend. That's what I think it will feel like.

'My images of retirement come from my family, and they are not what I want for myself and my friends', says Rachel E who works as a cataloguer and part of a team creating a national database for libraries in Australian schools. She likes to imagine herself in around five years' time: 'not working at all, though not retiring from life'. However, she also plans to think about 'life beyond independence' and to 'take steps to cover that probability'.

Some people anticipate there will be problems and plan ways to avoid these. Richard S, a self-employed technology and educational consultant in Birmingham, United Kingdom, who has not yet retired, and his wife, Tamsin, already retired for five years and who works from home, have plenty of room in their home, but are worried about the impact of suddenly being in each other's 'space': 'Our worst fear (we hope!) is of finding we are on top of each other'. To avoid this they have pre-planned an unofficial post-retirement agreement (not quite a pre-wedding nuptial arrangement) that they hope will help them work things out amicably.

Many people think they will include some work in their lives after retirement to keep themselves 'connected'. Plans can be specific ('They have said they'd like to bring me back for particular projects'; 'I plan to open a coffee shop – no stress'; 'I hope to retire with a hobby in tourism') or vague ('I might look around for something'; 'I'd thought of working as a postman part-time').

Some cannot imagine life without work, whether or not it is paid work, and those who think in this way tend to think that the difference retirement will bring for them is that they will choose the nature of their work and the frequency of their leisure time.

Some of those in their thirties and forties, with whom I talked, tended to take the view that retirement is such a long way off it is hardly worth thinking about. Women in this age group said things such as: 'I can't really imagine it at this stage'; 'Don't ask. I've no idea'; 'I'll be doing things I like, I guess. But I wouldn't know.'

Robyn B, married with three children, and currently a Brisbane technology consultant thinks that if she were to be asked in 10 years' time when the children have left home about what she'll be doing in retirement, she may well have a different answer from now. But at the moment she imagines she will use it to focus more on her own neglected 'not enough time now for' interests. As someone who has a family, works full time, and has also studied during most of her career, she is well aware that 'women are used to doing more than one job at once', and suspects this influences how they envisage their lives in retirement.

Sam P, a lawyer, and Heather P, a public affairs manager, both in their late thirties say they don't yet know what life in retirement might mean for them, but they have already made a significant change to their work patterns to accom-modate sharing the responsibilities of raising a family. Now that they have two young children they have changed to working four days a week and each spends a day looking after them. Their innovative approach to work practices suggests they may have less difficulty in adjusting to retirement than others who've not made such changes.

Retirement seems a very long way off for Roddy C, who has been a butcher in Sydney since he turned 14. He is now in his mid-forties and married with three children. He says: 'At this point in time retirement is the one thought that is furthest from my mind'. He knows his super will 'call me to stop doing what I have done all my life in 21 years time', but it is not a prospect he welcomes. 'I'll miss the screaming of the children, the banter of the locals, the old folk telling me just what it's like when you retire', he explains. He enjoys his job and has watched many butchers who retire keen to return only weeks later because they miss the company and the physicality of the job.

When contemplating the future, the males in this age group tended to imagine themselves still engaged in 'work' of some kind and even bringing in income. Nick H, in his mid-forties, and an Australian engineer based in Asia, puts it this way:

> Everyone dreams of making a lot of cash and retiring on a tropical beach with a pina colada. But having a laptop on the beach to do some computer design, writing, or other work would keep the brain in tune. I don't actually think of stopping work, only getting to a time where work is optional and I am doing something I really enjoy that is both of interest and brings in income. I would like to have a nice workshop with lots of great tools and equipment to build things I have designed.

When I asked Nick if his generation sees things very differently from the generation that is retiring now, he replied:

> Slogging on while plugging small contributions into a retirement fund happens less these days. People are more adventurous in terms of career risks and generally jump jobs for salary increments rather than spending long years with the same company. On the other hand, the generations are probably not all that different – people's dreams are pretty similar.

Adrian D, who is in his late forties, and the managing director of a company based in South East Asia that provides educational outreach and exhibitions in aerospace science, takes a similar view:

> In today's job market and especially in South East Asia there is a very different mindset to the issue of retirement. It seems that the new generation of workers shift regularly from one job to another. I don't see a great deal of attention being paid to preparing for retirement. Personally, I have never considered retirement as a defining point in time where one should 'down tools' and start planting roses. I will never 'retire' as such because I consider life as an opportunity for work, exploration and learning that should continue until the very end.
>
> I would love to have a small business serving visiting amateur astronomers and enthusiasts in what is now termed astrotourism. I still have a keen desire to travel, and feel driven to explore as many places as this planet has to offer. And I would dearly love to travel into space and see the earth as a whole. This may be possible …

Wanting to retire as soon as possible is what motivates 33-year-old Bruno B. He works intermittently for large banking corporations in Australia, and likes to organise his working life so he can take blocks of time away from work, even up to nine months at a time. When I asked him why he does things this way, he explained:

I have to work very hard as an operations manager and after a heavy bout of working I need time out so I can come back to myself. At first I sleep for a long time and then slowly I begin to feel better and I begin to explore the things I am interested in. I can go into them in depth then. It works well for me.

The option of cycling between work and leisure in retirement, a pattern identified as ideal for baby boomers in the Merrill Lynch survey referred to in Chapter 1, is something 33-year-old Bruno, from Generation X, is pursuing as part of his working life. It is clear that younger generations already employ a diversity of work patterns and that if they are able to conceptualise retirement, they think about it in relatively non-traditional ways.

Reality check

When those who are retired look back and compare their present realities with what they imagined retirement would be like, verdicts range from those who find it just as they had predicted ('almost exactly as I expected'; 'just as I expected'), to those who find it quite different. 'An unrealistic image of myself living by the sea, and reading all day' is how Ceridwen C, formerly a journalist, and then a French and English teacher, recalls her expectations of retirement. 'How could I have been so blithe and irresponsible?' she asks ruefully.

Hugo D, an associate professor of mathematics at a Sydney university says, rather Irishly, that he 'really had no expectations of what retirement would be', but it turned out to be 'not quite as I thought it would'. The 'not quite as I thought' part is a fairly common experience – sometimes it proves better, sometimes worse, and at other times just different. Melissa K, who ended her career in a marketing role in a company in Perth, made a comment echoed by several others: 'I worried that I'd be bored to death, but I find I am enjoying just relaxing and doing a lot of reading. It is rather a nice surprise.'

A former professional rugby league player both in the United Kingdom and Australia, Marcus H, always imagined he would spend his retirement travelling to see all the major sporting events – he'd go to the Superbowl for the gridiron, to the World Cup for the rugby and so on. However, this isn't what has happened. He finds that he doesn't want to spend his life with huge crowds and the threat of crowd violence, and he doesn't want the trauma and expense of regular world travel. Instead, he watches these events and a whole range of other sporting programs on the television, a much better arrangement than he'd anticipated.

These accounts, reinforced by others described further on, suggest that there can be a considerable gap between how people imagine they will feel and act in retirement and how they actually behave. Many people surprise themselves with the way they react and the activities they find themselves pursuing. But it is all rather unpredictable. While some fear the prospect or ignore it altogether, the possibility of realising dreams and doing things you may never have had the time or opportunity to do before remains an attractive lure.

Taking the plunge

What motivates people to make the shift into retirement? They may think and plan for it over the years, but how do they actually choose the moment when they will turn prospect into reality? Having enough in the super fund is probably the most commonly mentioned motivation for taking the plunge. But people don't always understand what leads them to choose a particular moment in time.

Pierre Trudeau, a former prime minister of Canada, made a sudden decision in 1984 to retire from politics at 65. It was a decision made after what he describes as a 'long walk in the snow'. The story goes that he had taken his sons to judo, come home, walked alone in a snowstorm until midnight, then returned to take a long sauna before bed with the decision made. His resignation as Canada's prime minister was announced the following morning.

Other politicians such as Victoria's premier Steve Bracks and Queensland's premier Peter Beattie, both in their early fifties, also resigned unexpectedly. Bracks says the decision took him around two weeks, citing family-related reasons that made it difficult for him to continue to commit to public office, while Beattie says he decided to retire after almost 10 years as premier because he realised he was 'over' politics.

Sudden decisions that take even those who make them by surprise are not uncommon. Jessie B, a managing editor at a Canadian publishing firm, recalls her decision vividly: 'My decision to retire came very suddenly while sitting in the garden with my sister who was visiting from England. It was just days before our daughter, Lily, got married. My sister was surprised and sceptical but I didn't change my mind.'

Tom N, an academic, found himself telling his boss about his plans before he'd articulated them to himself:

> I'd given very little thought to retirement and was half surprised at myself when I suddenly announced to my Dean at a party that I thought I'd give the game away in six months from then. A few years before that I'd been to a retirement seminar and was shown a video of oldies engaged in apparently pleasurable activities – one woman was working a spinning jenny and a chap was cleaning the bottom of his boat with great pleasure. That had put me off retirement for a long time.

For many people there is no surprise involved – they plan their retirement meticulously, considering all the relevant factors before choosing what they see as the right time. They may stage this to suit themselves, their family, or even their organisations. Others shilly shally around with the prospect of retirement but can't make up their minds to take the plunge. Ian McKellen, well known for many of his acting roles, but particularly for his role as Gandalf in *Lord of the Rings*, thinks he'll probably make a gradual exit. In an interview in *The Good Weekend*, 26 May 2007 he explains:

> I think what will probably happen is I'll take six months off, and then I'll discover that I've had a year off, and then two years, and I will think, 'Oh, I seem to have retired'. And the idea of never working again isn't a horrific one; in some ways I would be rather relieved.

Taking a long time to come to a decision to leave a career behind is not uncommon. The media is fond of analysing the dilemmas of sporting stars who agonise over whether or not to retire from their 'game'. My young brother, a soccer player, 'retired' from soccer on several occasions. I remember my mother, who followed his career avidly, phoning me on at least three different occasions to tell me the deed was done: 'Mark's hung up his boots for the last time, Don', she would say. I wasn't even sure what she meant the first time, not having heard the expression, but I could tell from her tone that it was something she thought of as momentous.

When you are propelled towards retirement by circumstances out of your control you are likely to have rather different feelings about the prospects retirement holds for you. Ill health can play havoc with people's dreams, as can losing a partner. Experiencing corporate burnout or being made redundant also takes away all sense of control – something that can be very difficult to handle. Others find themselves in situations where they feel they must retire even though they hadn't planned such a move: 'My son needed me to help with the children after he lost his wife'; 'My mother had to be cared for and there was no one else who could do it'. These experiences colour people's attitudes as to what retirement will mean for them.

Up until an accident with a chainsaw that caused serious damage to his arm and prevented him from continuing to work in a factory environment, Ricky D had a career in technical and operations management. After the accident he accepted a role as technical adviser to the pharmaceutical industry in Australia. I talked with him just a week or two before he was to 'retire' from this position:

> I am leaving, or more correctly, being made redundant for financial reasons. In many ways I feel my worth to the industries in which I have worked for the past 43 years is being jettisoned. Interestingly though, since the news of my imminent departure has spread, I am being asked to participate in a number of major initiatives. Mind you they want me to help, but as yet [they] have not offered me any money for this.
>
> I am looking forward to the release from stress, but the unknown does cause me apprehension. It will change my life, of that I am sure. I have had five major surgical operations in the last seven years. This is always in the back of my mind, and I feel I need to run fast to do the things that have been on my 'gunna do' list. It's time to do those things that I like, such as getting back to doing

woodwork. I'm already going to classes – in a timeframe
that suits me.

Ricky's frankness about his situation and his philosophical
attitude suggest he has a good chance of enjoying his
retirement, but there are others in similar or less palatable
positions who take their 'exit' badly and, not surprisingly,
find it difficult or even impossible to shrug off the negative
feelings the experience causes.

~

Imagining retirement is easy at one level – dreaming dreams,
being set free from the constraints of a working life. At
another level it can be difficult to envisage what you will in
fact do in the day-to-day reality of the time that lies ahead.
Discrepancies between imagined versions of retirement and
real experiences suggest people's expectations are often off
target. This isn't really surprising, as societies have done
little to promote the importance of thinking about what
retirement means and how to 'spend' it for the best return.
Compare this with the efforts made to encourage people to
prepare financially, or to look after their health, and you'll
notice the difference.

Not everyone welcomes the prospect of retirement, but
most people look forward to the advantages it might have
for them when the time is right. Some hold on to the idea
that it will be a time when you can realise your dreams;
some see it as a time when the pressure will be off and you
can live more as though you are on holiday or in the mid-

dle of a long weekend; others think things won't be so very different but hope you will be able to reorganise your life to make it possible to do more of the things that matter or are important to you.

How do the early years of retirement measure up to these predictions? In the next chapter we listen to what people think, feel and do in the first three or four years of the retirement experience. We hear their stories from the 'inside' and see what the implications are for life in the twenty-first century.

The
early years

I celebrate myself, and sing myself

'Song of Myself', Walt Whitman, 1855

Cathy Freeman, the Australian Olympic gold medallist, described how she felt in the first few years after her retirement from athletics – a rather different kind of retirement, but one that nevertheless vividly dramatises how it feels to retire from something that has been important:

> When I quit running, a part of me died and I grieved for a long time… It was the one sure thing in my life. No matter what else happened, running was always there, was always real… I felt like I was lost in one of those blow-up castles that you see at kid's birthday parties and somewhere out of sight a giant was shaking the foundations so I could never find my balance… I had no idea where I belonged or even who I was anymore… I knew myself as one thing – a

champion. I had no other identity. I had to reinvent myself or I'd be lost. (AAP, 18 February 2007)

Finding a new identity, creating a different life, dealing with loss, fearing the future – all issues Cathy touches on – are part of the transition and adjustment process for those who are retiring from a lifetime in the workplace. In this chapter you will hear how men and women initially react, how they adjust to their new state, the thoughts and feelings they experience, and what they find themselves doing in the first few years of retirement.

Initial reactions

When you first retire you no longer have to travel in the rush hour, you leave behind many of your responsibilities, and you look forward to the freedom of a kind you are unlikely to have experienced before. You have a window of time to adjust to your new status in the eyes of society and you can think with pleasure about the possibilities that lie ahead. Is this what happens? In some ways it is.

In most cases when people first retire they have an extraordinary sense of elation. Shedding the symbols of the workplace is a pleasure that is often emphasised. Dancing to the tune of others and dressing in suitable clothes (uniforms; 'power dressing'; suits) becomes a thing of the past. 'No alarms, no traffic, no ties, no shoes', recalls a cheerful Adam T, previously an industrial chemist. Libby T, a former school secretary, says she traded in all her office clothing, then 'took off her stockings and left them off'. She says she 'felt a little bit sexy at first, but as familiarity grew the feeling slipped away!' Henry W, previously a publisher, and Meg W, who worked in communications and fundraising, have taken to writing books since they retired. They say they sometimes don't get out of their bathrobes until two o'clock in the afternoon, and very much enjoy not setting the alarm clock.

Crystal C left behind a high-powered administrative position and also shed some clothes: 'I refuse to rush off anywhere ever again unless it is an emergency. I sold or gave away all my work clothes and will never wear another suit.' She was ready to end her career because the workplace had 'got too mean for me'. She retired at 62 after 30 years working as an office manager in the State of Florida. The position she held involved a wide range of responsibilities, including liaising between the president of her organisation and a staff of hundreds. Her work had recently become more highly pressured because of changes that had resulted in the organisation becoming larger and more corporatised. She welcomed her retirement with infectious enthusiasm: 'I had the most exquisite feeling of freedom, which I still have. My husband, Len, says I had my conscience surgically removed and he may be right. I loved my job but it was stressful and I was ready to have a different life.'

My own reaction to retiring was a little muddied by immediately going overseas for our US house swap. Yet the knowledge of my new state was something I hugged to myself with some degree of awe. It was a bit like the way I felt when I first discovered the existence of the local library as a child. When I borrowed my first library books I walked home holding them close, a little afraid someone would come out of the library and take them back. Being retired and able to spend my time as I choose seems almost too good to be true and I half expect someone will come and tell me to return to work. My sense of pleasure and relief does disappear from time to time, but then it washes over me again and I can't believe my good fortune.

Enjoying the prospect of endless time to do what you want is another common theme in people's initial reactions. Carrie T, who taught Middle school in Washington, United States, sums it up this way: 'I had a wonderful sense of time spreading out without all the stress that accompanies a working day'. Mitchell N is ecstatic about not spending time in peak hour traffic and having that time for his many interests. A rather perverse pleasure I heard about more than once was that of staying in bed and listening to traffic reports on the radio. As the M4 or the A4 or whatever route you normally follow becomes more and more tangled with traffic, satisfaction and contentment mount!

Heavy responsibilities other than those created by the workplace are sometimes acknowledged as intruding, but nothing really dampens the feeling that a 'myspace' has arrived. I was often reminded of the opening line 'I celebrate myself, and sing myself' in Walt Whitman's poem, 'Song of Myself', when I was listening to people glimpsing a future where they imagined themselves exploring and expressing their personalities unfettered by the restraints of a working life, and perhaps realising new selves.

'I keep thinking it's Saturday'

How long do these euphoric feelings usually last? For some they are short lived. According to Julia N, 'the euphoria lasted around eight months'. Others say the feelings never go away. 'I still [after four years] wake up with a smile every day because I don't have to get up and go to work' says Crystal C. And Carrie T, in spite of minor reservations, agrees: 'I feel relaxed and on a holiday. Every day is Saturday! It is the best time of my life (Now, if only my knees were better, my weight lower, my chin firmer, my eyelids higher…).'

The theme of life in retirement being like an extended weekend ('I keep thinking it's Saturday') comes up frequently. 'You can read the paper every day – every day is like the weekend – you can do all the things you do then all the time', Adam T reports with the kind of tangible enthusiasm that should be bottled! He was diagnosed with multiple myeloma shortly after his retirement, but even so his delight in the freedom from the constraints of work is powerful medicine. The pleasure in his newfound freedom remains undimmed by the difficulties of his illness, which he sees as a quite separate issue.

Over time most people find snatches of their original pleasure recurring. A recent cold, wet snap when I was able to stay reading in bed instead of joining the traffic brought a flood of warm feelings about being retired in its wake. At the same time a multitude of contradictory thoughts and feelings characterise most people's transition to retirement. Alongside the pleasure and relief is the sadness of saying goodbye to a way of life, to friends and colleagues, and to the readymade status you once had as a useful member of society.

Regrets, doubts and anger

The important transitions we all experience – starting school, beginning a new job – usually involve some misgivings. Leaving the workforce for a life of 'retirement' is not very different. Even when you are delighted to escape from deadlines, timetables and overwork you are likely to wonder whether you've made the right decision, and if so, whether you've made it at the right time. You will, after all, slowly slip away from the radar screens of your colleagues from the moment they offer their warm, envious congratulations, if not earlier.

Amy H had mixed feelings when she retired in 2006 from her role as an English and history teacher. Amy met her husband Ray, an Irishman, in Toronto where she had been teaching and they lived in Ireland for ten years (Amy did a degree at Trinity College, Dublin, during this time) before returning to Australia with their three children in 1983. A nasty accident, causing Amy to fracture her pelvis, tipped her into retirement:

I felt very, very sad about my decision and could hardly bring myself to tell my Year 11 students I was leaving. At the same time I felt relief, an 'I'm free to smell the roses' feeling, a feeling of being in charge of myself.

I found I was very tired and I wanted to think of my first year as a time off. I have lots of plans about things I want to do in the future – knock down our house and rebuild, have an extended holiday overseas to celebrate our 40th wedding anniversary, follow up on family connections with the Irish involvement in World War 1 and so on. But so far I seem to be in a state of flux.

Regrets about loss of contact with communities and networks of colleagues, and more particularly, friends who are a part of the former workplace, are common in the early years of retirement. 'It was the most disorienting experience of my life', says Brenda S who gave up a full-time academic position at the same time as moving interstate with her husband, Jordan. I found many references to grief peppering what people have to say about missing their contact with workmates ('I had a period of mourning'; 'I felt real sorrow…'). Another cause for regret is recognising that the particular skills you bring to your work will no longer be in use – you will not be needed in quite the same way ever again. Just days after her last sociology lecture, Diana O touched on these themes as she described how she felt about leaving the workplace: 'My contribution as a good teacher, as a passionate performer will not happen any more and I mourn the ending of that. I will miss my students, the emails they send me, my time with them.'

The early stages of retirement can also aggravate feelings of self-doubt. Julia N, who left her position as a researcher for a big daily newspaper in Sydney about two years ago, finds retirement better than expected, but also finds it confronting to be asked to reflect on her feelings and thoughts. As she explains: 'When you get down to the nitty gritty it is about facing the fact that one is no longer a spring chicken.'

Julia is enjoying retirement and finds herself doing things she wouldn't have done earlier such as travelling to Asia independently of her husband, Cameron, who is not yet retired. But at the same time she is juggling with other more unsettling insights: 'I have always felt a bit irrelevant and one of the uncomfortable things about this period is that it makes me feel even more so, which is not such a nice feeling.'

Dominique D is another person who finds thinking about retirement troubling. As she says: 'I'm not where I want to be within myself, and I don't think I know where that is'. I felt moved by Dominique's words as they seemed to erupt from a painful place she didn't often visit. Leaving her work as a drug counsellor in Adelaide three years ago had been an unhappy experience for her, and though it was she who'd resigned after 25 years with a government authority, she felt as though she'd been catapulted into leaving. She was unhappy about the restructuring that was undermining things she'd cared about and nurtured for so many years: 'I hadn't any image of retirement. It came upon me suddenly. I felt angry that I'd left the way I had. I felt diminished and I still feel angry when I think about it.'

Anger or disappointment with repeated, unnecessary and stressful change in the workplace is often cited as a reason for choosing to retire at a particular point in time. Without that impetus many people say they would have stayed on much longer. Guy M, who held a managerial position in a large Sydney bookshop, found his feelings of sadness at leaving tempered by his annoyance with the behaviour of some of his superiors in the organisation. Barbara N, who left behind an executive leadership position and responsibility for around 100 000 employees at a telephone and communications company in Greenwich in the USA, says she retired in 2002 mainly because of 'merging mania' – corporate cycles of downsizing and merging. As a result she was required, among other things, to write manuals for managers to help them cope emotionally, and this sort of thing finally propelled her away from her work. Her desire to escape became stronger than her need to stay. Issues of status that had been of concern to her were soon outweighed as she began to realise 'success in the public world is too demanding'.

Loss of identity

What is it that people miss most about their working lives? A loss of identity is fairly high on the list. Julia N sums up these feelings after spending a lifetime in the workforce:

'I am not sure of what to say about "who I am" as I am no longer defined by my work'. Many people work for forty years or more so the connection between your working self and your sense of identity can seem more or less set in cement, particularly when you are doing something you love or think is important. As Detective Briony Williams in Jane Goodall's *The Calling* says, 'Life was work, work was life' (Hachette Livre Australia, 2007, p. 170. Reprinted with permission).

The question as to why some people suffer more than others from feelings of a loss of identity is difficult to answer. Sometimes a person's professional self is so intermingled with their sense of identity that it becomes impossible to separate them. As Hugo D explains: 'My problem is that I'm a man who has always been defined by my job. So it's really important to me with anyone I meet for the first time to tell them something like "I'm a mathematician at the university. At least I was. I still teach part-time etc."... I need this to exist somehow.'

A very high proportion of the people I spoke to think men suffer more frequently and more profoundly than women from feelings associated with loss of identity. Perhaps this is natural, given that it is only in recent decades that equal opportunity in the workplace has been in vogue. Robyn B thinks men suffer more for a different reason: 'Women have had more practice at reinventing themselves than men. Think about it. Women change their name if they marry, they begin careers and then may become mothers, so they have to leave and rejoin the workforce at various times. Men usually have far fewer sea changes and so are less practised at creating new identities.'

Many factors play a part in determining the degree and nature of the sense of loss people experience. The length of a working life, how all-consuming it has been, the circumstances of leaving, even the weather – all can play a part! Bill G, a chief operating officer from a large corporate firm in New York, links having retired (or having 'been' retired, which he says is much worse) with feeling a loss of self-worth. He says that people's questions compound the problem: 'They ask "what do you do all day?" And they don't mean to make you uncomfortable, but you don't know how to answer. In fact, I think they're thinking, "What will happen to me when *I* retire?"'

Bill points out that if you are without hobbies and your main interests are sporting activities, being retired in New York is not such a good option. The extremes of weather make things like running and outdoor tennis impossible at times. He found himself turning to voluntary work (around six hours a week at a Medicare Rights Centre and later on a Suicide Hotline), partly because it was a way to contribute to people in need, partly because it filled in the time, and partly so he'd have something to say when asked what he was doing. In other words, it provided him with a ready-made identity. As he says: 'Voluntary work gives retired people some structure to their days, but it also gives you a sense of belonging to an organisation. Retirees miss that sense of camaraderie.'

When asked to talk more about his feelings on the subject of retirement, Ian H, a corporate worker, showed quite a lot of hard-headed resistance, not to mention deflection: 'When I try to front up to defining my attitude towards retirement, I find myself recalling the answer a doctor friend of mine gave about his attitude towards exercise: "I usually just sit down and wait till the feeling goes away."' Eventually he acknowledged being retired does have some difficulties:

> I felt a strong sense of displacement and disempowerment in the early years of retirement. Well, I'd spent 30 years in the firm as a senior manager, and I had a lot of say in what was happening – especially in what was happening to me! Although I have been let down gently by being given some part-time work, people are now inclined to put me and my requests on the backburner.

'Your sense of self comes from what you do', says Dominique D. In her job as a drug counsellor in Adelaide she felt productive and useful. Now she says she doesn't know anymore how she fits into society. She finds life a bit like 'an endless holiday'. That has its advantages of course, but it is not how you want to live all the time. Dominique enjoys retirement, particularly since becoming a grandmother ('I was surprised at how important it is ... it feels so good'), but she is still a bit lost and guilty about not doing more with her own life. She found some recent voluntary work helping Serbian refugees with their conversation skills satisfying, largely because she was able to help them cope with their feelings of displacement. This was reminiscent of her counselling work. She hopes more work of this kind might help her get back the sense of self that seemed to disappear when she left work.

Not everyone experiences strong feelings of identity loss when they retire. Melissa K, a former secretary to a government official in Western Australia and later a telemarketer with a Perth newspaper says: 'I never thought working was an important part of my life. It was a job that paid me and I was good at it and found talking to people fun and interesting. I carried on so long because I knew no other way of life.' Don N, a recently retired pathologist, who says he spent most of his life 'institutionalised' (boarding school, national service, hospitals and so on), says the camaraderie of the workplace was never an important part of his life, and he doesn't think he'll miss it. 'I'm happy in my own skin', he explains, acknowledging that being retired makes you feel less important, but Don says that he can live with that. He likes being at home where he can live 'an intelligent internal life'. Similarly, Carl T, a former assessor in aged care services feels no hint of identity loss now he has left that career behind: 'I don't need an identity. I've had all that. I'm comfortable.'

Another high flyer who says he can't claim an identity crisis is Ross H, a former senior lawyer at a major cultural institution in Washington. He puts this down to the fact that he'd been successful in the workplace over a long period and he didn't really feel any need to go on with that life. Ross retired at 74, although because of new policies he could have stayed on longer if he'd chosen. Instead, he was happy to be able to make a greater contribution to the running of the household so he could better support the career of his wife, Penelope, as an art critic and writer. As he points out, she had previously supported him in his career for over thirty years.

When I asked Ross what else was important to his life in retirement, he drew from his pocket a small handwritten diary (he has never learned to work with computers, relying instead on secretaries). It is in this that he records his children's birthdays and makes lists of what he and his wife are doing each day. In his case this includes sitting on various local and national boards.

I was interviewing Ross in the sitting room of his home in Norfolk, Connecticut. It looked out on to a vast expanse of grassy meadow that fronted on to a lake. To my delight now and then a hummingbird would flash by or land briefly, wings whirring. A little earlier we'd been consulting a very old bird book of Ross's. I'd noticed pencilled lists of birds seen on various dates and learned that Ross had recorded these sightings as a young boy. As I listened to him talk about how truly devastated he would be if he lost his diary, I couldn't help thinking of Wordsworth's thought about the child being father to the man.

The way Ross orders his life had been established very early on – a sense of priorities over show or display. He knows what is important to him, he knows how he likes to do things, and that is perhaps part of why he is so at home and comfortable now in retirement.

~

When retirement is closely followed by a partner's illness and death it becomes difficult to assess how much of the deep sense of loss that is experienced is due to leaving work. David M, a pastor for the Seventh Day Adventist church in NSW, who suffered just this fate, does his best to untangle what he missed about his previous work from other feelings:

> The whole dynamic of family relationships changed, but it is difficult to sort out those changes due to retirement itself, and those due to the ill health and death of my wife.
>
> I did not miss about 85% of work-related features, but there were a few aspects of my previous work that I did miss to some degree. There was a sense of being out of the loop with reference to work experiences. But my biggest sense of loss in this regard has been not being able to share my knowledge, skills and experiences where they could benefit people.

There are, of course, those lucky enough to avoid regrets, doubts and anger. According to Crystal C, 'I've had none of those feelings whatsoever! I am free to be me and I don't have to request annual leave for trips and I don't have to evaluate anyone or anything.'

Going back to work

Work can be addictive – a hard habit to kick. Those who find that hard work brings personal rewards often find it difficult to short circuit their connection with work. After retirement these people usually reproduce their working lives in some guise or another. They don't get a chance to feel fully retired because they go straight back to work.

I recall my astonishment at the behaviour of a friend and former colleague, Tim M, in this regard. A departmental staff meeting was held the day before he was to leave us. Tim actively contributed to that meeting, saying things such as, 'It would be good if we could...' or 'Why don't we try...' as though any future plans were of vital interest to him. He was about to retire, but it was as if he were in denial. He'd not let go of the idea that he was part of the place or its future, an attitude I found both admirable and bewildering. Some years after his 'retirement' his wife Lorna told me it hadn't taken Tim long to begin working more hours than ever before, taking on consultancies on everything under the sun. 'I thought of myself as being retired, but I literally worked my heart out', Tim admits, acknowledging that serious ill health was a consequence of his actions. 'Do you know why you work so hard?' I asked. 'Not really.

Humans aren't rational, are they,' he replied with a grin. He now runs a cattle property in southern New South Wales.

The pattern of leaving the workforce and then beginning work in an entirely new enterprise or 'career', yet still thinking of yourself as retired, is becoming more common. Mervyn N, in the financial services industry, and Lara N, a teacher, both loved entertaining, and were 'famous' for their dinner parties and hosting charity evenings in their Sydney home. They decided to try running a B&B and Lara used the Internet to search for a property: 'We found it, saw it one day and bought it the next'. They love their new lifestyle and talk about themselves as though they are retired, though 'not in the image of the retired people you see on television advertisements' they hasten to add. Perhaps they'll never retire in the traditional sense because they seem to connect purposefulness with pleasurable 'work'.

On the other hand, people sometimes say that they are not retired when in fact they are (in terms of the usual definition). On several occasions I talked with wives who told me that their husbands had retired and then I talked to the husbands who said they hadn't retired yet! When I asked the husbands about the discrepancies in what I was being told they usually smiled and explained it was because they didn't want to be thought of as 'old' or 'finished'. As my husband said to me the other day when I was doing my usual probing about why he doesn't acknowledge that he's retired, except rarely or in unusual circumstances: 'There's a social stigma attached to saying you're retired. Also, it is conversationally disabling – people don't quite know what to say if you say you've retired.' A good answer I have to admit, though I must say I'm still saying 'I've retired' with naive delight and rushing on into an account of what I'm doing.

Carl T has a particular spin on not working – while his wife, Liz, a full-time librarian, refers to him as being re-tired, he says he is 'on sabbatical'. Carl has worked in civil aviation, as a patrol officer in New Guinea, and over the last ten years has held various roles in aged care – challeng-ing, tense work from which he wanted to take a break. From his perspective retirement is something he might come to in the future, but in the meantime he plans to take sabbaticals between taking jobs that keep him physically fit and ac-tive. He has learned from his work with aged people that mobility is the single most important factor in maintaining quality of life. He says he would have no difficulty taking a job as a handyman, for example, because he recognises the value and usefulness of such work. Six months after our interview Carl got a job as a storeman and packer. He says he finds it physically demanding but that's just what he wanted.

Many people like to feel they still have a foot in the door of their workplace. Making a slow exit ('I faded away') by helping a replacement into your job, or organising part-time work you can continue after you leave, provides ways to make the break less irrevocable. Understandably, the motivation for returning to work tends to be strongly re-lated to financial matters, although keeping in touch with colleagues and the mainstream are also cited as powerful motives. Another strong influence is the desire to hold on a little longer to an identity forged over the length of a working life. Sometimes offers to go back to work prove too good to refuse, as Craig A found when he was asked to 'help out' at his old reinsurance company by doing some part-time work in Asia over a three-year period. His wife had not yet retired, he loves travel, and he now had time for his golf, so he was happy with this arrangement.

According to Ernestine N, the sense of loss is more manageable if exiting from the workforce is a gradual experience: 'It makes the break between 'working' and being 'retired' less noticeable, and the benefits/drawbacks of both states are then fairly easily sorted out'. Ernestine retired twice, first from a position in the Adult Migrant Education Service and second from head of studies in an English language centre, with extensive and demanding volunteer work both between and after her full-time jobs: 'You can see how a state of "gradualism" has to be factored into my reactions. Feelings of loss applied only spasmodically and seem, in retrospect, to have been only slightly concerning.'

Sometimes people plan to do some part-time work, but gradually find the idea loses its appeal. When Sandy C retired from Sydney's Department of Main Roads in 2003, he thought that first he would tame his 'feral' garden, paint the house, do lots of fishing, and 'plenty of nothing' for six months, then he'd do some part-time work. He devised a witty business card to announce that he would still be available for consultancies. It carries all the usual details of name, qualifications and contact details, but these are superimposed on an image of white sands, lapped by a soft blue sea that mirrors a stretch of blue sky. An empty, low, white, slatted wooden chair sits facing the sea in this idyllic scene. The card amusingly evokes the ambiguity of both wanting and not wanting to work once you are retired.

As it turned out, Sandy didn't do many of the things he'd planned. 'I haven't once touched a fishing rod', he says. He has done some part-time work 'in concentrated bursts', but he adds that work is beginning to lose its appeal and he may not do much more of that either. Instead he finds himself looking after a website for a geographical society, doing voluntary work related to projects on Sydney's transport future, and absorbed in sorting and restoring 50 years of photographic negatives taken in 1952 in the United Kingdom and Germany by his father when he was in the army. 'It's what my wife calls "fiddling around"', he explains.

Guilt

People often refer with a smile to the protestant work ethic to explain their long hours of work, or alternatively to explain the guilt they feel when they think they're not working hard enough. The phrase has even fallen into football commentators' vocabularies: 'That was a great goal. It was his "work ethic" that did it. He didn't give up for a minute. Kept working and got his reward' (Channel 7 AFL commentary 2007).

I was talking over lunch with Liz T about the power the work ethic still has to create feelings of guilt. She thinks it may be losing its grip at last. She watches her daughter's cohort and their attitudes to the workplace, and finds them quite different from her own:

> Our parents went through wars and the Depression, and instilled the idea of the almost sacred value of work into their children. Today's young people have grown up with the knowledge that the jobs they will do in the future are probably not yet invented, and change is the order of the day.

Some people have worked out wonderful ways to manage guilt. Crystal C had hers 'surgically removed' you'll recall, and Carrie T, the former Middle school teacher, makes a fine show of rationalising hers out of existence: 'All I do is enjoy myself. It's rather selfish, but since teaching was such a "giving" profession, I'm not feeling guilty at all... Next year, I tell myself I have to "buckle" down and start contributing to society and get serious.'

In Alfred Jarry's play, *Ubu Roi,* Pa Ubu has a trick of packing his conscience away in a suitcase when it confronts him with uncomfortable truths about his past deeds and his character and behaviour. The most recent generation of retired people, including the early baby boomers, are so steeped in the protestant work ethic that such a deliciously appealing solution to guilt anxiety is not readily available for them. But maybe there's some hope: 'I still feel uneasy about wasting time, but I'm getting better at it', says Avril P.

When I talked to Brett C, a Melbourne solicitor who has made several attempts at retirement, about the feelings that accompany retiring, his first word was: 'GUILT'. It was a knee-jerk reaction and obviously something that troubled him. I interviewed Brett (on a weekday…) in his newly built home in a country club complex in the Yarra Valley, Melbourne. We were enjoying the view from the living room of beautiful green paddocks dotted with trees and an ancient-looking horse that he and his wife, Emma, had christened 'the ornament'.

Although Brett and Emma had downsized from the family home to their present location, and Brett had 'begun' to retire a few times, so far he'd 'shied away from the big step'. Brett takes his responsibilities to his clients very seriously, though he frankly confesses that 'the ego massage of being so needed, so busy, so little time on my hands' is part of this addiction.

He explained that it wasn't that he especially liked his job – he'd never really liked the Law, but had found he was good at it – that kept him on the 'squirrel wheel' he'd constructed for himself. The hardest thing for him in planning to retire was the feeling that he ought to be at work all the time. When he began to cut back his hours and take some leisure time, to become seriously semi-retired, people reinforced his guilt feelings by making friendly comments such as: 'Taking the day off?'; 'Home early?'; or 'Not going in today?'

Later, while driving us to the station at around 5.00 p.m. to catch a train back to Melbourne, the route took him past his old office. The lights were out. Brett was visibly distressed at the sight: he couldn't believe that no one was there at such an 'early' hour, as he would have been. Brett kept looking at the office to see if he'd been mistaken – confirmation, if it was needed, of the powerful grip the protestant work ethic has when it gets its claws in deeply. Although not everyone articulates their guilt feelings as clearly as Brett, he is certainly not alone in experiencing self-reproach when he stops 'working'.

Hayden K, a New South Wales farmer in his early 70s, has a slightly different version of this. He is doing less physical work than he did in the past, but he still experiences terrible guilt feelings unless he is actually 'in the paddocks'. Working in the office just doesn't count for him as 'real' work, even though, as Hayden explains, he is probably more productive and useful there than when outside.

My own feelings of guilt bubble under the surface if a day goes by without my doing any writing, for example. I seem to have a ledger buried in my conscience that tells me what counts as legitimate activity. Gardening, exercising, going to the library, and writing of any kind get my stamp of approval, while too much time spent shopping, cooking, talking on the phone or having lunch out don't get a guernsey. When my daughter was visiting recently she asked why we had stopped getting the newspaper delivered. 'We waste too much time reading it', I replied. 'Mum, she said in exasperation, 'You're retired!' Guilt, whether related to needing to behave in particular ways, or to frittering away valuable time, is experienced and talked about by retired people almost as much as the joys that leaving work behind can bring.

Patterns of behaviour

In the first year of retirement people often seize the moment to do something on a grander scale than usual. It might be holding a big celebratory party, taking a trip that has been only dreamed about, or moving house to be near the mountains, the sea, the grandchildren, or other family members – or just to get far away from the rat race.

A surprising number of people give a party not long after they retire. Zoe N gave a big sixtieth birthday party 'to celebrate the end of an era'. She added 'I feel fairly sure I'll never want another like it'. Carrie T held a large holiday party, making all the food herself for 80 people – 'the biggest one I've ever done'. Kelly and Simon M enjoyed a ruby wedding celebration with the family coming from around the globe to join them. This latter event was timed to coincide with their moving house, and the party became 'an activity which somehow made it easier to dispose of the family home and move on with the kids in full understanding, if not in total agreement'.

People also choose this time to travel, particularly in a way or on a scale they haven't attempted before. House swapping across continents, a year-long trip exploring surroundings, major road and camping trips, or 'motor homing' are some examples. The timing is often deliberate. As Crystal C explains, she and her husband organised 'a five-week car trip beginning the day after I retired, so I never felt like I was waking up to nothing'; and Craig A was ready to set off with his wife on six months of travel around Australia the very moment she retired. He collected her from the gates of her workplace and they drove off into the sunset.

Moving house is something else people plan to coincide with the beginning of their retirement. In a sense, this decision sets in train how the early years will be spent. Packing up the old home and getting the new into order has its own imperatives. Moves aren't always for happy reasons. After the death of his wife, David M, the pastor, found himself adjusting to a 'nomad' type of lifestyle. 'Instead of a stable and continuing home life, living with a lifelong loving companion, I now share what feels like, at least at this early stage, a transient "home" life with my two daughters in particular, and their husbands.' He is happy and busy in that life, but it isn't the life he was looking towards.

Most people, though there are exceptions, think that having some kind of structure to their life in retirement is important. They rejoice in the fact that they can create a plan that will work for them. This doesn't mean they follow it rigidly, and in fact being able to deviate from the 'rules' without any form of punishment hanging over their heads is part of the pleasure.

When you are at work you often put certain things – sorting the family photos, reorganising the toolshed, getting the address book up to date – into the category of 'things I will do when I retire'. You imagine you'll have the time and the inclination then to do these tasks. Often they don't get done, or at least not in the first few years. Comments such as the following are typical: 'Well, I did plan to get my house in order – clean out closets, organise shelves, maintain a neat desk. Did I do these things? No!'; 'I must admit that a few of the household practical jobs I planned for years to do after retirement are still looking at me waiting to be completed.'

Some people plan to do what they have always wanted to do, but find events intervening. Jessie B, who retired from the position of managing editor in a Canadian publishing firm in 2006, says: 'I had two or three things in mind that I wanted to do. Nothing terribly ambitious – I wanted to finish my degree, something I did part-time when we had lived in Guelph. I wanted to run a 10 km race. Spend time gardening. Ski more often. Kayak on a regular basis. Add something else to my volunteer list.'

The death of Jessie's brother in the United Kingdom at the end of 2006 meant she spent a lot of time travelling back and forth during his final illness. She also travelled to other places for various reasons, and for a time events seemed to control her rather than she them. Now she is beginning to fulfil some of her earlier plans. She has joined a running group to train for the 10 km run, for example, but wonders whether there may be more things in store for her that she'll discover as time goes on:

I think I am aware that it would be easy to mosey along without much thought to taking control, planning, and doing some of the things that make you realise you are 'living'. I have on occasion asked myself – after reading that a middle-aged woman just did some amazing feat – whether there is something yet to be identified that I would like to accomplish. For the moment, my wilderness kayaking gives me that sense of adventure and survival.

Others make an effort at structure because they feel better when their life has some definition. Julia N, who describes herself since she retired in 2006 as 'just be-bopping along as usual', recognises that without some structure to her days she might 'drift into an isolated space'. She adds: 'I try to organise one external activity every day. Could be going to the Pilates class, or picking up my friend's children. I also try not to organise too many things in a day because then it feels the same as when I was working and I get extremely cranky.'

Hugo D says he is aware of the dangers of being without a structure to his days. But in his case it is inevitable:

My life is bound up with my wife's, and her career is all-consuming. So there is not really any structure possible. It's a problem to me. Theo S and Edward M (two now-dead colleagues) were talking with me at a party years ago after their retirement. Each of them said they had a problem with finding a reason to get out of bed in the morning. I mean, why should they? I don't have that problem really because of 36 years of running every morning. Still I understood exactly what they were saying... I can't just curl up my toes. On the other hand, I don't feel like embarking on a new career in a B&B or a chicken farm somewhere.

Getting physical

Another observable trend in what people do when they first retire is to spend more time on sport or exercise. There is a strong awareness that getting fit improves the quality of life, and with several decades of retired life ahead, people want to be healthy enough to enjoy them. According to Harvard Medical School's Health information website:

> Retirement is a luxury our great great grandparents never dreamed of. Around the turn of the [twentieth] century, the average life expectancy was 47. People quit working only when they were too ill to keep going. Retirement for them signalled the end of life, not merely the end of working life.
>
> Today, 70 percent of Americans will celebrate a 65th birthday, and the fastest growing part of the population comprises those 85 and older. People spend more years in retirement than they do in childhood and adolescence combined. How to spend that time has become a very real concern.

Similar trends in ageing populations are evident in many countries. While few remember their parents or grandparents taking a lot of exercise, almost everyone interviewed mentioned their own turning to more regular exercise after retirement: 'Well, I always begin with exercising'; 'I attend my aerobic dance class four times a week, and on the others, I walk on my treadmill'; 'I'm playing golf more often' and so on. Others take on projects that involve other kinds of physical effort such as helping with environmental restoration. Tom N, the academic, was motivated in the early years of his retirement to help out with the project to restore a site, overgrown with lantana, where Australian impressionists such as Streeton and Roberts had camped, after he learned the grandfather of his wife, Ernestine, had been part of the establishment. The Curlew Camp Artists' Walk now links this restored area to the ferry at Taronga Zoo, a route visitors to the camp used in the 1890s.

Yoga, too, comes in for high praise, not only for its physical benefits, but for its spiritual, meditative and calming side. Crystal C, who you'll recall swore off wearing suits after she retired, found she likes the venue with 'its wooden floor', and really likes the kind of people who do yoga. 'The people are just themselves'. Barbara N, the former US executive, began yoga because of stress-related back problems. She thought she would like to teach yoga after her retirement, and worked towards that with the idea of building her own small-scale business. In fact, she found herself involved in a frenetic whirlwind of activities, and took a while to realise that this was 'not fun'. It was the 'be still' concept of yoga that helped her sort this out and scale back. Now she has her yoga classes taking a central place in her life, and finds she can prioritise her interests and other activities more selectively.

Saul T, a builder in his sixties who plans never to retire, says he nearly lost his father, a builder, because after he retired he 'gave up being active and didn't give up the morning and afternoon teas'. Saul and his wife now also run two exercise venues that are doing very well. They are specifically for women who spend 30 minutes on a variety of machines to improve muscle tone, bone strength and achieve weight loss. Venues of this kind have sprung up all over the world in recent times and people of all ages, including a surprising number of those interviewed, use them regularly.

The heart of the matter

In times past when there was a comparatively short time ahead after retirement the question of how to use that time was less pressing. But now a longer period awaits and the question of how you will use that time certainly arises. For some it is a relatively easy decision – they go on doing what they have always done though in a different context. Jan E, a medical technologist, told me about her old boss, now in his eighties, who carries on his research into lice, a great nuisance in the sheep and kangaroo industry, in his garage 'out the back', and continues to make important discoveries and contributions to the scientific world. Many people continue with their professional interests in some way or other, though some professions are better suited to this process than others.

This isn't true for everyone; in fact, agonising over how best to spend the new time at your disposal is an underlying theme that keeps recurring. Julia N puts it well:

> I have a lot more time to think and feel, which is good and bad – sometimes it clarifies what I want and at other times it illustrates that I don't know what I want. I am spending much more time thinking about my life and what I want to do, in the short term as well as the long term, and sometimes this is uncomfortable.

Some people count activity itself as a sign that they are using time well. As a former sportsman, Marcus H says, 'I'm always doing something. I'd feel guilty if I wasn't'. When pressed as to why this is, Marcus wasn't really sure – he just knew that was how he felt. On the other hand, some people discriminate between the kinds of activities that 'count' for them and those that don't. Kevin P, the former Jesuit priest, admits he cannot read fiction before 5 p.m. because that's a discipline with which he's grown up. Pieter P says that for him it's out of bounds to go to the movies in the middle of the day. 'Why?' I ask. 'Because that is when I used to be at work,' he replies. Pieter ranks other things he does such as reading the papers, managing his investments, or learning a language, as more acceptable things to do in the daytime.

Understanding what motivates your choices of how you

use time after you retire is extraordinarily complex and related to individual beliefs, values and circumstances. We may not be conscious of the reasons behind our choices: they are not the type of thing you write in a list. And yet they are at the heart of the matter. We each have inner knowledge of which activities will make us feel useful and purposeful. I know writing, reading fiction and doing a painting (not something I do well, but it doesn't seem to matter) are at the top of my list. If I don't do those things I'm not really happy doing all the other things I want or need to do. But I'm not entirely sure why this particular set of activities are at the top of my list or what might replace them if my circumstances were to change.

Many people find that having what can loosely be described as a project, doing something that uses individual skills, interests and abilities to create a result you personally rank as worthwhile, achieves that sense of purpose that otherwise can be elusive. Projects can be grand and challenging; for example, learning to play all of Beethoven's concertos, attempting a PhD, writing a biography, building a collection, holding an art exhibition, or teaching at the Open University. Or they can be simpler in scope, as, for example, becoming involved in a bush care project; joining a group ('I swore I'd never join a book club, but it's the best thing that ever happened to me'); developing new skills ('I've learned to create DVDs of recent trips I've taken – The Baltics, Berlin, Cuba…'); or returning to old pastimes ('I resumed piano lessons and try to practise an hour a day'). Over time, pursuing these interests shapes people's lives in new ways, and provides them with the 'new' identities they need for feeling they are making good use of their retirement.

What, then, can be said of the early years of retirement? The sense of freedom and joy that comes from being 'released' from work is celebrated and enjoyed by most people and can be found intensely exciting – it is often long lasting. There may be regrets for the past, and guilt attacks that niggle away. Anger, too, at how you may have been treated, or at injustices you have witnessed can be painful and difficult to combat.

Feelings of self-doubt and loss of identity run like a subterranean river through some people's days. This creates serious problems of disorientation and unhappiness, though with time people usually find ways to deal with the issues involved. As always in life there can be sudden un-expected blows that turn up in the form of health problems or the death of someone you love, and they usually fall more frequently at the retirement stage of the spectrum. Yet treatments are improving, there is greater hope, and more people are recovering well. People are extraordinarily resilient in dealing with problems of this kind.

You are also likely to find that retirement doesn't turn out quite as you thought it would. You probably won't complete all those banked-up tasks, and you may well turn to activities you hadn't anticipated. You'll probably do more exercise and you may also go back to work perhaps full time, but more likely part time or just for a while so that you still keep that precious feeling of being 'retired'.

Choosing what to do so you don't feel you are just filling in time is another important concern. Finding your 'balance', as Cathy Freeman describes it, is crucial, but it is likely to be something of a juggling act as you come to terms with the changes in your life. When you find the balance that is right for you, living through the early years of retirement in the twenty-first century can be full of promise.

Relationships in retirement

Will you still need me, will you still feed me,
When I'm sixty four?

'When I'm 64', Lennon/McCartney.
Published by Northern Songs/Sony/ATV Music Publishing

The greater longevity and better health people are experiencing in the early twenty-first century is responsible for many things. Longer marriages, for instance. At the beginning of the twentieth century the average length of a marriage before one partner died was 28 years; now, in this century, it is more likely to be around 45 years. In other words, the married relationships of people after retirement can often involve almost as long a commitment as ordinary marriages did in the past. In a poem written in 1821, Percy Byshe Shelly gloomily referred to marriage as 'the longest journey', a phrase that became the title of E. M. Forster's second novel. Today, the longest journey is very much longer.

Having a long time ahead in your marriage provides new challenges for relationships. When today's more relaxed social and cultural attitudes to relations between the sexes are also taken into account, it is evident that partners in retirement will have many new fronts to negotiate. People divorce more frequently, marry more often, have blended and extended families, and have parents and grandchildren to look after. Both partners are likely to have been in the workforce and they will need to forge new identities, separately and together in their retirement. How are their responsibilities to be shared? Who will end up doing what? How can identities be developed in ways that keep relationships intact?

The longer lasting retirement also brings an additional edge to questions about people's domestic roles in the marriage relationship. In the past, when a shortish span of life remained, the roles of retired partners tended to remain much as usual: Wives doing the cooking and housekeeping, husbands mowing the lawn and attending to hobbies. But radically altered ideas about gender roles have carried over into the sphere of relationships in retirement and old paradigms are dissolving. This creates new issues for partners to resolve in their retirement, issues that wouldn't have arisen previously.

When one retired partner is more entrenched in older traditions than the other they will have different expectations of each other's roles in their relationship. Resolving these tensions is quite a challenge, as the idea of the female succumbing to the male's point of view (honouring and obeying) is no longer necessarily seen as a virtue. Even when both partners share the more relaxed attitudes to conventions of the modern age, as many baby boomers do, the cultural and social changes of our times continue to create new challenges and issues for them to face. In the following pages the ways partners are dealing with their life in retirement, the issues that arise, and the solutions that are found are put under the microscope.

The order of your going

An important factor influencing relationships in retirement is the order in which it takes place – 'the order of your going', to use Lady Macbeth's words, or the pattern of your exiting. A common pattern is for a husband to retire to a wife who has stayed at home, or has retired previously from part-time or full-time work. The pattern of the wife retiring after the husband is less common, though becoming more so. This latter trend is partly because women from the generation before the baby boomers would often join the workforce quite late after their children were grown up. Their delayed start may have involved updating earlier training, or beginning a new career, and retiring a little later. Another pattern is for couples to exit the workplace together.

Personal space – too little of it – is often an issue that arrives with an unexpected wham when couples retire whatever the order of their going. When they retire at different times there is an 'invader' and an 'invaded', and the impact is sudden and can result in severe skirmishes, even war! When both retire at the same time they have to negotiate how to occupy the new order without getting in each other's way. Battles over 'territory' are out of kilter with the dreams and hopes of the newly retireds, so tensions may be repressed or running high.

The invader usually brings a legacy of the customs and attitudes of the workplace, a place they may have occupied for 40 years or more, into the home; the invaded fears disruption to their routine and a loss of control over their life. The problems that arise vary in seriousness for cultural and social reasons, and because of the different personalities and history of the partners. In the past, these problems have often gone unacknowledged, been kept in the closet so to speak, but this is beginning to change.

In cultures where traditional patterns dominate, the likelihood is high of the wife feeling that her world is being invaded on her husband's retirement. In Japan, for example, social and cultural expectations have long been strongly geared to the man having his 'empire' at work, while the woman's domain is in the home. There are variations to this pattern, of course, and recent social changes – such as some young women resisting marriage and avoiding childbirth, intent on finding greater self-fulfilment, are beginning to have an impact. Nevertheless, Japan has witnessed the emergence of a 'retired husband syndrome' (RHS), identified in 1991 by Dr Nobuo Kurokawa. This syndrome involves Japanese women brought up to believe in the man's superiority becoming quite literally ill after their husbands leave the workforce and move into 'their' space (often already relatively confined, given the size of a typical home in Japan). Barbara Lawrence, an academic researcher in Boston, claims RHS affects around 60 per cent of wives who suffer debilitating physical symptoms that include: 'stomach ulcers, slurring of speech, rashes around the eyes, growths in the throat, palpitations, tension headaches and depression', as well as 'agitation, gas, bloating, muscle aches, and other symptoms of stress'.

Blue funks and other stories

Isamu M, a young man who lives and works in Tokyo, explained the phenomenon of RHS to me in the following way:

> My father's generation had to work hard to rebuild Japan after World War 2. They spent long hours at work and didn't have much time left over for personal life – their company had become their life. So, after they retire, they don't know how to spend their time without friends and hobbies. Then husbands stick to wives and wives get sick. In Japan, this social phenomenon is called *nure ochiba*, which means 'Wet leaves stick to broom'. Many people in Japan who retire from a company seem to feel loss, and sometimes such people get into a sick, blue funk. Although this hasn't happened to my father, my mother [Sakiko] wants to make sure it doesn't happen to her.

Isamu's account helps to explain the unflattering terms such as *sodaigomi* (oversized garbage) and *nureochib* (wet fallen leaves) that I came across in articles reporting how Japanese wives are describing their retired husbands. But Isamu talks about both parents' need to adjust to their new situation, and so I was interested to hear more from his parents' perspectives. As neither Kazuo nor Sakiko M speak English, it was arranged that we would use email for my questions and Isamu would translate their replies for me. The picture that emerged is an interesting variation on accounts available in the media.

Kazuo M retired ten years ago from his company position in Tokyo as a driver for executives, a difficult, demanding job that required him to leave home early in the morning, often not returning until midnight. He is glad to be free from the stress, the need to be punctual, and the long working hours. He now spends his time caring for his family: 'I work for my family instead of working for the company. For example, I give my family a lift somewhere, clean the house and so on. The structure of my days follows my family's everyday life.' He does manage to include his hobby of fishing quite often in his schedule – a great pleasure for him.

Sakiko M works part time, about 18–24 hours per week, as a building cleaner in Tokyo. She still works because, as she says, 'I don't want to spend all the time with my husband. If I stop working, I am very afraid I will not have any connection to society.' There are few jobs for aged people in Japan. Sakiko says she is not looking forward to retirement, and wants to keep working to stay involved with her society for as long as her body will allow her.

People around the world delay retirement for fear of the adverse effects of being in too close proximity to their partners. Angus R, who has been retired from his career as a lawyer in Chicago for almost a year, confesses to two major fears: 'I thought there was a danger that I'd get in my wife's way and also that my ego wouldn't be satisfied. Fortunately, I've been able to transfer my working life into other interests, so my fears proved unnecessary.'

In the June 2006 Donington Report, published by the Donington Group Pty Ltd, Hugh Mackay argues that the phenomenon of RHS is widespread in Australia: 'the wives of newly retired men ... complain of the flagging energy of their retired husbands, at a stage of life when they themselves are feeling more liberated.' 'I feel as if I'm on the up escalator and he's on the down' reported one of the people Mackay interviewed. Amy H reports that to avoid a situation of this kind her husband plans to keep on working: 'He's wise. We both need space. We'd kill each other if he were to retire,' she adds cheerfully.

Toby C, who was retrenched from his job as a fitter at a Sydney company ('it took them three years to sort things out and the staff talked about nothing else for all that time'), took up paid gardening six days a week. He doesn't ever want to retire, though he wouldn't mind cutting down a bit: 'My wife and I don't have the same interests. I like camping and outdoors things, she likes cruises and watching TV. We're opposites. We'd drive each other mad.'

Another complaint I heard recently from a retired wife was of excessive sexual demands from a husband with time on his hands and access to Viagra. The more frequently heard complaint is 'I married him for better or worse, but not for lunch.' As Molly A says, 'Owen retired 20 years ago. Now he waits for me to cook his lunch and dinner. When am I allowed to retire?' Stay-at-home wives get a bad deal here.

Him to her

Margaret P is an example of a wife who was at home when her husband, Charles, retired, though she'd reluctantly left behind her career as a primary teacher apart from occasional part-time work, because of major surgery and the health problems that followed. My interview with Margaret and Charles took place in the living room of their Sydney home – a tranquil, welcoming place with photos of their adult children and grandchildren suggesting the importance of family in their lives. There was also a vase of magnificent velvety red roses in the corner of the room.

Margaret's reaction to Charles's retirement from teaching in 1988 was vehement: 'I absolutely hated it. It interrupted my life, and my routine, after so many decades of the home being my space where I followed my own methods. It was an invasion. I still say after 20 years "I wish you were at work"'. I looked apprehensively at Charles to see how he was taking this, but was reassured by his smile. 'Don't worry.

She's nice mostly! I quite understand her feelings', he adds. Some partners can be honest with each other, even in front of other people, without it affecting the basis of their relationship, a fact that continues to surprise me.

Margaret went on to explain how wrong she thought it was that Charles had to retire on the day he turned 60 – the New South Wales Department of Education policy of the time. It made her angry to think someone of his experience and worth could be discarded just like that. She also explained that in spite of the close relationships she has with her husband and four children, she is essentially a solitary person. 'See that green chair outside', she said, pointing to the window. 'My son bought that for me for Christmas many years ago. It cost $25 and he earned the money for it from pumping petrol in the school holidays. I sit in it so I can see people passing and watch the traffic. It takes me outside and I read there and stay in it for three or four hours at a time. I like my own company.'

Charles had a long career in education, culminating in his role as the headmaster of a large Sydney boys' school. He, too, had felt anger about the policy that led to his retirement. When I asked him about his reactions he emphasised the strangeness of shifting from being someone important in many people's worlds to suddenly being 'nobody':

It was unbearable for the first few days. You are too young to give up work at 60, and in some ways I found my feelings about it got worse as time went on. You begin to perceive what other people think of you when you are a retired person. They just think of you as old. And you fear you will lose your ability to stand up and be yourself. I did overcome this in time. I was asked to run the Higher School Certificate examinations at several places and that gave me a way of getting back into the world. I'm nearly 80 now and still doing that. I keep trying to retire from it, but they won't let me!

Charles explains that during his career he developed a successful small publishing business, so that it was not such a financial burden to pull out of work as it might have been. Working as a headmaster, writing and taking care of his publishing concerns, teaching migrant education classes at night, and doing some coaching kept the family income buoyant, but meant that he and Margaret spent very little time together. And as she explains 'Both our mothers were widowed and weekends usually involved visits with them'. Charles adds dryly, 'We did get to watch television together on Sunday nights. But of course we didn't talk to each other even then.'

As time moved on, Charles says he began to establish a different routine that took him out and about – to bowls, on regular camping trips to go fishing with his two brothers ('the trips took six months to plan and six months to recap'), to meet up with a group of former principals for lunch each month, being on selection committees, and his occasional work running HSC examination centres. Margaret concludes, 'I have gradually come to accept we are a couple in retirement together. But it was wrong, that policy!'

As I was leaving I commented on the roses. 'He gave them to me,' Margaret says and I catch a very friendly, loving look pass between them.

Some occupations still retain a policy that sets a compulsory retirement age. Pilots usually have to retire from flying at a specific age, and in some countries members of the armed forces have to hand in their badges when they reach certain age limits, as do detectives. This latter fact has caused Ian Rankin, author of the *Inspector Rebus* series of crime fiction novels set mainly in Edinburgh, 'in real time', something of an unusual problem. The main character, Detective Inspector John Rebus, is aged 40 in the first book published in 1987. This means that, according to Scottish law, when Rebus turned 60 in 2007 he had to leave the force. No more novels with Rebus in his usual role were possible. Fans were devastated. An MP in Scotland, herself a devoted fan, approached the Minister for Justice about the possibility of changing the compulsory age of retirement for detectives to 65, just so Rebus could carry on with his career. She was not successful!

Hilary N retired from her job as a kindergarten teacher and had two glorious years at home. Their children had left home and Hilary was ecstatic about the freedom retirement represented. But then the tidal wave hit: her husband, Hugh N, retired and was at home everyday and expecting lunch. Hilary's disquiet had nothing to do with not loving Hugh or with not wanting to be with him – it had to do with a feeling of her life and space being taken over. He brought his company work mentality home. Hilary felt he saw her as being there exclusively for him: 'He wanted to own me and my time'. It was also to do with their different personalities and perceptions of retirement. She saw it as a time of 'joy, the first time I'd been free in my life; freedom I'd planned for and wanted.' Hugh saw it as representing the end of something important. 'I'm finished', he would say.

Hugh was a 1950s man with a mother who didn't really acknowledge that Hilary worked. He hardly noticed that she had worked either, as her school hours meant she was at home for him when he returned from work. When Hugh was 58, and not wanting to retire at all, he was asked to leave his company. After this, Hilary's experience of retirement became quite different. According to her, Hugh remained in denial about his departure from work for several years. She saw him fighting his demons, finding ways to keep up a front with others, not really having strong friendships of his own, and letting his hobbies lapse. Hugh had always had secretaries and after he retired, perhaps subconsciously, he expected Hilary to take on that role. He thought she would be there for him most of the time.

Hilary realised they had to turn what had been a 'weekend relationship' into 'a week plus weekend one' if they were to find a better equilibrium. She set about finding ways to share her network of friends with Hugh. He's since joined a tennis club and meets up with the husbands of some of Hilary's female friends more often now. They also sold their second car to make room in the garage for Hugh's hobby of carpentry. I saw some of his beautiful work after our interview – ships in bottles, furniture for his grandchildren and so on.

When Hugh was diagnosed with Parkinson's disease in 2005, Hugh and Hilary realised this had been an un-recognised factor in his behaviour over the previous ten years. They offered their cooperation to researchers in the hope of helping the medical world find out more about the disease; so far Hugh is managing well. Hilary is also more adjusted to their new state and is enthusiastically following hobbies of her own, including researching social and family history. Hilary's experience is fairly typical of women who have managed to both work and run a house-hold and family before retirement, though not everyone is necessarily as resourceful as she and Hugh have proved to be in dealing with the issues that arise.

Her to him

When wives retire after their husbands, different syndromes come into play. I remember the early months after I retired involving a kind of silent struggle as to who was setting the agenda of our days. I was anxious about what my husband's reaction would be when I was going to be out day after day during the week. As Tony is the cook (and a great one) in our family, for us it was more of an 'I'll be out for lunch', rather than a 'What's for lunch?' problem. He felt I was at home at last, so why did I keep disappearing? I love being at home with him more than anything, but I felt I had to resist this view of things. (I just rang a friend, and her husband, Daniel, picked up the phone. 'Sorry she's out', he answered. 'Now that I'm retired she's always out', he added. This made me feel much better.) There were genuine reasons for my being out a lot at the time, but I realise now that I was also afraid of losing the sense of independence and freedom that comes with working. Now that we both understand this better, we sort things out more easily, but the struggle between us did go on for some months and still recurs occasionally.

Crystal C, the administrator from Florida, whose husband, Len, works at home, was worried there would be a change in the equilibrium of her relationship when she came to retire:

> My husband was a little concerned that I would drive him mad as I have always worked away, but it has been just fine.

This is in part because we have a large house and I have the upstairs for my computer and a 'room of my own'. We let our house cleaning person go, but my husband vacuums and I do the rest, though not very well or often and we don't care!!!

Jessie B, had similar fears when she left her Canadian publishing firm: 'The first adjustment was for Dick to get used to my being in the house on a regular basis. It took a little while, but eventually he was able to get on with his work and leave me to do whatever I wanted to do.'

Some men who retire before their wives aren't entirely clear about what they're going to do with themselves when they're at home alone. Jim G, a woodwork teacher in Sydney, retired in 2002 ('I was sick and tired of 34 years of red tape'), while his wife Beth, a history teacher, was still working full time. After Jim made the decision to leave work, people constantly asked him what he would do with himself. It made him anxious and concerned because he really had no idea what he'd do. He decided to say he'd be doing nothing. And for a while that is exactly what he did. At times he felt lonely and bored. After a life spent talking to people all day, he suddenly spoke to no one. Beth says she came home from work: 'feeling rather like the men you see in the movies who want to sit and read the paper, recover and not talk to their wives'. Jim would be there, waiting to have his first real conversation of the day like the wives in those same movies.

After two years Beth decided to retire, partly from guilt

that Jim was at home by himself. She recalls the moment in 2004 when she told Jim of her decision. To her astonishment he didn't look too happy. He'd adjusted to his life alone in the daytime, had found things he enjoyed doing and liked the routine he'd fallen into, which included travelling to America for four and five weeks at a time to teach woodturning to groups of retirees. According to Beth, Jim had 'become set in his ways', something with which Jim agreed. Email connects him to the world at large, and this along with the sports he pursues, his publication schedule, his American trips and their five grandchildren make him think that maybe it's time to 'retire' again.

While I was talking to Beth and Jim in their living room I noticed that their grandchildren's heights, reaching 193 centimetres for the eldest, are marked in pencil on the dining room wall. I've now introduced this practice to my grandchildren. When they arrive from Brisbane they head to the laundry wall to be measured and to see if they've grown.

It is Beth now who sometimes struggles to find her 'space'. She also feels she left work too early and misses teaching, even grieves for it at times, though she says the longer she's retired the easier she finds it to leave those feelings behind. She thinks a good way to approach retirement is to see it as having stages. You might worry you should be doing some voluntary work or beginning a course you want to do, but it helps to realise it may not be the right stage for that. In her view, learning how to banish guilt makes things easier for everyone.

Examples of men who retire and then support their wives' careers is a pattern more commonplace than it used to be. Mack B describes two of his friends following this path in recent times – one resigned to be a house husband for his wife, who is an artist and set designer, and another to support his wife, an opera singer based in Germany, who travels to opera houses all over the world. The latter husband likes to set himself reading projects and has taken up translating jobs (a novel from German to English, for example) as a way of keeping his own interests alive. Feeling that you have lost your identity or submerged it in your partner's is clearly a danger in this situation – a danger many women would say they know all about, having played that role to their husbands over the years.

According to Abigail Trafford 'Post-retirement marital malaise' is a syndrome to which US males are particularly vulnerable. 'In the nation's capital, where workaholism is prevalent, a person's identity is mainly rooted in a job title. When the big job ends, he may wonder: Who am I?' Trafford recognises that wives in the workforce, particularly the baby boom generation, can be in a similar situation. 'So there is his retirement and her retirement, the impact of his retirement on her and the impact of her retirement on him, and the impact of both retirements on the quality of the marriage. Many couples go through years of churn as they grapple with retirement issues' (*The Washington Post*, 25 October 2005).

Him and her

What of couples who retire together? Obviously they may have to make adjustments of various kinds, but does the fact that they are consciously organising their new life with each other in mind make any difference? Circumstances and personalities are so varied that it becomes difficult to generalise, but in my experience couples who arrange a joint retirement and plan a new life together (it usually includes a house move) feel they are setting out on an adventure that helps them avoid some of the inherent problems. As Kelly M, who retired at the same time as her husband, Simon, and immediately moved house, says: 'we enjoyed the fun of setting up a new residence; being forced to sort out our belongings and get rid of unwanted items; and having a chance for a fresh start perhaps'.

A joint retirement was decided on by Edna M, a psychologist with a strong interest in the arts, and Matt M, a professor of chemistry. Edna says they saw their retirement as 'a lovely empty space we'd fill with activity'. They acknowledge their different personalities and interests – she is outgoing and finds friendships central to her enjoyment of life; Matt is more self-contained. Soon after retiring they decided to move from their Sydney suburban home to an apartment. Edna explains the impact of this on their relationship:

> Retiring at the same time, and having such a dramatic change has made our relationship if anything, better. This is for a couple of reasons – a new common project where we

are both novices; that is, we moved from living in suburbia to the North Sydney Central Business District. Also, the way of life here is so different – there is so little maintenance for us that we really can do more things together... I don't pretend for one minute we haven't had differences of opinion, but we've wandered through them ...

When Matt became ill and had his bypass operation, it was helpful for me to be close to the hospital, secure in a high rise away from the world. So we both feel we have done the right thing, and this of course makes us gentle and happy with each other.

Stories of this kind with different circumstances, emphases, and degrees of seriousness are unfolding in households around the globe. Some people solve their differences amicably, while others fail to find satisfactory solutions to the problems retirement can bring in its wake. Carol-of-the-epiphany found a way to avoid the problem altogether: 'I guess I have done the most unexpected thing of anyone I know. I left my husband after 40 odd years and have just bought a new house.' Deirdre Bair would see Carol's decision as part of the worldwide trend that is documented in *Calling it Quits: Late Life Divorce*. She points to the 'exploding phenomenon' of the increase in divorce among older people, and tells of those married for up to 40 and 50 years who are choosing this path in the United States and elsewhere.

Years of churn?

Once you are both retired and occupying your 'space' in the home, your relationship will have other changes to weather. You will no longer be drawing a salary and you will be operating within new financial arrangements and constraints; your readymade work identities will begin to disappear and you may begin to forge them differently or reclaim previous versions with a new emphasis; you will have more time available and will probably be spending your time, whether together or apart, in different ways and in taking on new responsibilities.

Are there 'years of churn' involved as Abigail Trafford suggests? What kind of personal and joint adjustments do the changes involve? To what extent do circumstances shape what happens? Does the pattern of who does what change at all? And what kind of strategies do people employ to help them cope with the changes that are taking place? I asked Mitchell and Katy N, and Jack and Megan H how their relationships have been affected by their both being fully retired. I interviewed both partners of each couple together, and in their own home, which created an interesting dynamic that became edgy at times, but was mostly good-humoured.

Mitchell N, who worked for a corporation in the food industry, and Katy, a journalist, came to Sydney, Australia, from the United Kingdom with their three children in 1978, expecting to stay for two years. Instead they ended up staying permanently. Katy retired in 1996, and a year later Mitchell, a general manager in his company, was retrenched. 'It was the best thing that ever happened to me', Mitchell explains, 'though it didn't feel like that at the time'. He says it wasn't so unexpected in the sense that in the 1990s once you were over 55 in the corporate world companies often removed a 'layer' of management. Sounds painful!

Katy's retirement was initially clouded by the unexpected – their daughter was involved in a serious accident, Mitchell was retrenched, and the dog died. Ten years on, retirement for Katy is 'absolute bliss'. She feels great relief to be free of the pressure of writing as a journalist, which she came to realise she'd found very stressful. She did an MA in literature, learned to play golf and bridge, is learning French, paints, goes to the gym, and does some regular volunteer work.

I'm conscious of how lucky I am and appreciate being able to financially support our lifestyle and being in good health. Being just a step away from life becoming dreadful is always at the back of your mind. But I don't really have a goal as I'm not one to look ahead or think about time very much. But now I have the time I want to be a better friend to people. I do think I was very self-centred in the career years.

Mitchell adds 'We suffered from the Yorkshire version of the protestant work ethic – the "where there's muck there's brass" expression originated in Yorkshire – and we grew up in a post-war generation that was used to a shortage of supplies and all sorts of hardship'.

Mitchell spent a lot of time writing job applications, over a hundred he recalls, and it was an anxious period for them both. He was then appointed to two federal government boards, going on to hold the position of chairperson of one of these for eight years, part-time work that initially took up to four days a week, but he tapered that down over time. Mitchell retired fully in 2006 at the age of 66. He says he thought retirement would have more negatives:

> I'd always wondered how you'd feel when you hung up your suit as it has such symbolic significance. I thought you'd feel that was it; you'd not be wanted again. But it isn't like that at all. It doesn't worry me an iota. I never touch my striped suits now. In fact, I've bought a lime yellow one I wear with a red tie that I wear if I'm meeting with someone.

Mitchell is a Francophile ('He read the whole of Proust in French,' Katy says; 'Took me 18 months', qualifies Mitchell) and likes living in France whenever he can. He attends the Alliance Française, does Pilates and plays golf, and has weekly music lessons (the clarinet is his instrument). Music is a passion. He had a band in the early 1950s called *The Red Aces*, and now plays both classical music and jazz. Retirement gives him more time to practise, and he and a female pianist are building their repertoire to provide music at functions (they practise at a dementia ward that Mitchell says gives real pleasure to both performers and audience). He believes you have to have a goal in retirement and his is to play Mozart's Clarinet Quintet at his seventieth birthday party.

What differences has retirement made to their relationship? Katy feels an 'earlier' Mitchell has somehow re-emerged in retirement. She watched the corporate world affecting him – a world run on fear, a world of grey suits worrying about how the rung above assessed them. She says Mitchell was much happier mixing with the country people he worked with on government boards, and that now he is retired his creative self is having a field day! She also acknowledges that she resented Mitchell's corporate self when she had to virtually give up her career (not to mention family and friends) to come to Australia:

> I lost my identity when I gave up tabloid journalism and left the *Daily Mail*. I stopped writing under my writing name Kate B – it was as if she'd died, and I had to pursue a different identity here. But now Mitchell is retired we are suddenly on an equal footing again. We're much happier.

Katy also feels she's become stronger as she's grown older, and that she is better able to stand up for herself within their relationship. 'Yes', says Mitchell, 'Katy even says "I don't want to go to bloody France again" sometimes. And we quarrel about politics. I'm decidedly left wing and she doesn't like the way I take the moral high ground.'

Mitchell agrees that they're happier together since retirement. He drew attention back to Katy's earlier comment about wanting to be of more help to her friends by addressing her directly: 'You say you don't have a goal, but really that's your goal. You have chosen to spend time with people you know who need help – we visit a friend with dementia each week, for example, and you see his wife a lot.' Katy, whose first husband died when she was 22, says that knowing what it's like to be in a lot of strife makes her feel able to offer useful support where it's needed.

They both think having a lot of space around you ('and greenery', adds Mitchell) is conducive to a happy retirement. 'We don't want to be a cruet set either – we've never been the "What's for lunch?" sort, and live fairly independent lives, except when we're on holiday and then we do lots of things together', adds Katy. As the interview drew to a close Katy commented she'd been really interested to hear what Mitchell had to say. This led them to reminiscence – half joshing, half proudly – about how they've known each other since they were teenagers. I'm hoping for an invitation to Mitchell's seventieth, as I'd really like to hear that clarinet concerto.

Bankruptcy made an extraordinary difference to Jack and Megan H's retirement plans, and consequently to their relationship in retirement. Jack had always been a careful financial planner and worked as a superannuation consultant before working in executive recruitment. The retirement he had worked and saved for was suddenly impossible, and he and Megan's plans for the future had to be scaled down.

Their misfortune arose when they invested their savings in their son's business, which was hit by the Asian downturn in 1997, resulting in their own and their son's bankruptcy. Luckily their home and an old weatherboard church they'd renovated in the Macdonald Valley in New South Wales were in Megan's name, but everything else was lost. It was a severe financial blow, but also a challenge to Jack's sense of identity as a successful businessman. For Megan, who'd worked as a milliner, brought up their three children and later worked in part-time jobs that used her craft skills, the fallout was also significant. Their son and two children (a third was born during this time) had to move into the family home for 13 months after his family was left homeless. It wasn't easy for any of them. There was not enough space and there were fears of recrimination and remorse. 'Fortunately, we adapted and managed to form scar tissue', says Jack in his dry way. Jack and Megan are now on the pension and trying to devise plans to get funds to travel overseas to see their daughter and her family who live in Singapore.

Both acknowledge the impact of this catastrophe on their marriage, and both have had many health problems to deal with ('our health horrors' as they describe them).

Their attitude to retirement is subdued. According to Jack: 'Expectations are technicolour and the reality is greyer, but you do adjust'. Megan says she feels guilty leaving Jack at home alone and she also misses having days to herself. Jack wonders what he'll do if Megan dies as he recognises that most of their friends are Megan's.

What do they do with their time? Megan is happiest doing creative things, particularly related to house decoration. She likes to work on her quilting and makes quilts for children in hospital with cancer. The housework is an increasing worry for her as her knee problems mean she has difficulty kneeling and getting down to do some jobs.

I guessed Jack would include reading and walking in his list of activities, as he's been famous in the local area for a quarter of a century or more for walking to the station, over three kilometres away, while reading a book. Reading, around five books a week, was indeed the first thing he mentioned. 'The day I couldn't read wouldn't be worth living.' He also walks everywhere. In fact, when we met for the interview he'd just arrived home from visiting his other son who lives several suburbs away – about a 14-kilometre round trip. Jack has an extraordinary gift of recall, a gift that sometimes surprises even him, and that he drew upon for his success on the TV program *Mastermind* as a competitor in the category of baroque music.

'He's very obsessive', says Megan, looking over at Jack who is pouring us a cup of tea and offering a plate of fruitcake. 'He makes his whole life about cooking. And he buys in bulk to save money. I'm afraid we'll end up like our friend whose garage is full of toilet rolls, cereal packets and baked beans.' Jack seems unphased by this revelation, as he does by all of Megan's revelations. He admits, yes, he does like cooking: 'I feel it's useful and I like the mechanical action of chopping up vegetables'.

They are a bit at odds about whether or not to move house and how they should structure their lives. 'I want to move to a smaller house and would enjoy decorating it, but Jack doesn't want to move as he says it doesn't make financial sense. I sometimes feel I've lost control of my life, I'm wasting it, and that we're living in a rut. I want to rebel', says Megan. Jack offers a different perspective: 'Life needs to have a pattern. We visit our "church" home at the weekends; we visit friends who live in the mountains and stay overnight; and we do our own things here. Moving doesn't make sense for us and we're managing well enough as it is.'

As they reflected on what they do with their time, many more activities emerged: they recently spent five days on a boat on the Murray River with friends, they are working on their plans to visit Singapore; and they enjoy helping out their children and grandchildren, and spend a great deal of time with them. I was interested in Jack's comment about their children's parenting roles: 'They do a much better job as parents than we did – fathers are around, there's lots more information about, and they're good at it'. Megan agreed wholeheartedly. It's unusual for parents to see things in this light. 'It doesn't sound as if you're in a rut', I ventured. 'Well, that's good news', Megan replied, 'I won't worry so much about it, then'.

There is plenty of evidence in all of these stories of the 'churn' caused by the various adjustments that partners have to make – to their new situation, to each other, and to the misfortunes life sometimes brings in its train, particularly at this stage of life. Yet for the most part a shared relationship in retirement can provide a kind of stronghold that helps partners to weather their difficulties; a time when they can reap the rewards of their companionship and rediscover what really matters to them both as individuals and as partners.

Moving on

The problems that emerge over time for retired partners can be problems that any relationship encounters – problems of failing to communicate well with each other, not managing to maintain individual identities within a partnership, not finding ways to divide household workloads satisfactorily and so on. But they are more likely to relate to the distinctive circumstances that accompany retirement: occupying the same space for a larger proportion of each day, having more disposable time, establishing different individual and joint identities, and finding new routines that accommodate the new way of life.

A number of ways of dealing with the issues that arise have been touched upon already. Identifying problems in advance, working towards a goal you want to achieve, developing a greater understanding of what is happening to you both and negotiating from this basis are some approaches that have proved helpful. Hugh Mackay suggests that a way of overcoming the 'What's for lunch?' problem is for men to engage in active psychological preparation for retirement. 'The challenge is not simply to fill in your time or "take up a hobby", but to establish a clear sense of personal identity that will avert your wife's risk of succumbing to RHS' – is the advice he offers in the June 2006 Donington Report. It is good advice for both sexes to follow, though just how it can be achieved by those who feel disempowered or lost after leaving the workplace does remain a mystery for some people.

Some see it as important for married people to keep up individual interests and to maintain their independence. As Pieter P puts it: 'I don't need to know what my wife, Heather, is doing or where she's going. And I don't expect her to be obsessive about my activities. We like to enjoy mutual interests, but we don't want to hold hands all day.' Marcus H thinks that you need to give each other space, and even though he is retired and his wife, Cynthia, is working, he encourages her to see her friends, and to do the things she enjoys alone in her time off. In his view they then better enjoy the time they spend together.

A practical course of action some take to prevent problems arising from too much togetherness is to pursue part-time or voluntary work. This allows some 'escape', a chance to get away for a time, but it also enables the one at home some time for themselves. Joseph A, a shuttle bus driver in Hartford, Connecticut, used to work for a large firm that built jet engines until he retired 15 years ago. Now he drives the bus from 7 a.m. to 3 p.m., three days a week. 'Boy you've got to get out', he says. 'And I like to give my wife a rest.'

A story reported in a local Sydney newspaper in February 2007 about Dennis W states that it was his wife who decided he should spend some time helping the elderly with their gardening. He earned a special mayoral certificate for his efforts: 'When I retired my wife didn't want me under her feet around the house, and she put me on to Easy Care Gardening. The people I work with are the salt of the earth ... there aren't many I wouldn't ride a porcupine bare-back for', he says with typical Ozzie humour.

After initial periods of adjustment to the shocks involved – and there are some – it does seem that most partners settle into a phase of life that has much to offer. This is not to gloss over the fact that most people are more aware than ever of their own and their partner's mortality, and that it can be a time of loss and uncertainty. But on the whole, most partners seem able to make the transition to a new life together, where they explore different aspects of their identities, do some of the things they've always wanted to do, and grow in the understanding of each other as they enjoy, even relish, their new state of being.

Even so, living in retirement with a partner means that there is a need to take each other into account when making decisions, and to make adjustments to allow for meeting one another's needs. Those who live alone do not have demands of this kind to consider on a day-to-day basis, but there may be other considerations that represent their particular concerns. In the next chapter we hear what retired singles have to say about the experience of 'going it alone'.

When I'm 64

Going
it alone

*To live alone is to be immensely in
charge of the silence.*

Michael Benedikt, 1999

Bernard Salt, an Australian adviser on demographic trends,
when asked to predict what society would look like in ten
years imagined a world where cashed-up singles would
rule the city. He suggests that after the nuclear family is
priced out of the cities it will be the singles who 'surge into
the social vacuum' (*Sunday Life*, September 2007). A large
proportion of that group will be retirees. It is predicted
that something like 58 per cent of baby boomers will be
without partners at age 65, creating larger numbers of this
new breed of singles than has previously been the case.

Singles today are acquiring a very different image
from that which attached to them in the past. The spin-
sters and bachelors who peopled my childhood, unmarried
aunts and uncles who wore dark all-encompassing clothes,

strange hats and went to church on Sundays, tended to be looked down on as a social group. It was a little shameful to be single then, especially for women who were often unkindly labelled 'old maids'. In the 1960s the stereotype was further confirmed by the popularity of The Beatles' hit song about all the lonely people, 'Eleanor Rigby'. The figures of Eleanor Rigby picking up rice in an empty churchyard, and Father McKenzie, alone in the evening darning his socks, come to mind. But now, remaining single is seen by many as an attractive option.

Some people choose to be single, some are reluctantly single, while others suddenly become single when a partner is lost to them. Some singles have never had a partner, some have had partners in the past, and those who have had partners may now have children and grandchildren. Some single people live alone. Others choose to live with family or friends rather than live alone, and even some who are not 'single' choose to live alone in a separate dwelling from their partner. This latter group live in different circumstances, close to, though not the same as, a retirement spent living with someone.

What does it feel like to retire and live alone? What are the pluses? Is loneliness a problem? What other issues are of concern? What do people choose to do with the time that is suddenly theirs? In the following pages retired singles provide some answers to these questions.

A tumbleweed existence?

In an online discussion on the retirement of singles, Ilene B writes: 'Although I am childfree by choice (and terminally single by experience), I do sometimes feel like a tumbleweed, drifting past others who have more roots'. How common is this kind of feeling?

Many of those who live alone are addicted to, and positively enjoy, the 'tumbleweed' sensations that life in this situation offers. Celebratory comments about the freedoms of not having to consider a partner's wishes, and being able to make your own decisions within the framework of your circumstances, chime long and often throughout interviews with people who live alone.

'I like living alone and am never lonely', says Raymond K, a NSW management consultant with a passion for cost accounting, who retired in 2004. Ellie P who retired in 1997 from her career as a social sciences teacher and who brought up her two sons as a single mother after a divorce, thinks living alone and being retired is the perfect combination: 'It is definitely the best time of my life'. A former seven days a week workaholic, Rose A, who opened what she says was the very first gift shop in Australia in Turnbull, Queensland, more than 40 years ago, says she'd had 'no idea what retirement would be like and never wanted it'. Rose lost her husband in 2001 ('I cried for two years') and was concerned about living alone without the solace of the workplace, but since retiring in 2007 finds she's 'as happy as a pig in mud'. She's redecorating her home, enjoying her garden and her grandchildren, and not missing work at all.

Others find the pleasure more of an acquired taste. Phillipa B, who was apprehensive about how different life in retirement would be when she returned to Australia from working as a linguist and Bible translator in Vietnam and Laos, says: 'I'm used to living alone now and enjoy being able to plan on my own for meals, when to go out, and what to do'. She works as an elder of her church, helping out in her community by doing things such as visiting people at a nearby boarding house who have mental health problems. 'I take my little dog who is loved by them', she adds. Leila J, who retired in 2004 from her position as an executive officer of a modern languages association in New South Wales, would agree with Phillipa's comments about the pleasures of living alone:

> [It] suits me just fine. In fact, I think it may have made me more selfish than I used to be. It is lovely to do just as you want, when and how you want to do it, to go where you want, eat when and what suits you at the time.

When contrasted with her latter years in the workforce, Ceridwen C says that retirement is a kind of nirvana. She didn't really like teaching, feeling it didn't suit her temperament. She was under great pressure in the latter years of her career with three teenage children to care for, elderly parents living upstairs ('my mother had a debilitating illness and I had the worst and longest menopause in medical history'), and a failing marriage that ended in divorce. But looking back after more than 20 years of retirement she acknowledges that loneliness is a significant part of the experience:

> The advantages of living alone are complete freedom and independence. You are not accountable to anyone, and are free to be your true untidy, erratic self. You don't have to tolerate all the irritating habits of a partner; in fact, you can become very selfish and self-centred. There's no one to shame or discipline you – you can leave crumbs in the bed, and eat when and what you feel like. Of course, you pay a heavy price – loneliness and the absence of companionship and love. Nothing is really worth the loss of this.

This brings to mind the other side to the coin of enjoying the freedoms that accompany living alone: the potential for loneliness lurking and waiting to catch you unawares. Peggy D worked for the American Institutes for Research, which took her to various locations, including a two-year stint in Egypt for the Ministry of Industry, until she retired in 1998. She now lives alone in San Francisco and admits to feelings of loneliness, though she is actively engaged in a range of activities including reading, walking and exercise classes, getting absorbed in political activities, attending concerts, visiting children and grandchildren 'both in and out-of-state', and doing volunteer work on community boards. 'It does get lonely not having someone to talk to', she says, 'particularly since for years I lived with a daughter and her family, helping to raise three grandchildren. That house was constantly full of life, and the first of those grandchildren has gone off to college so it is like a double empty nest feeling.'

In 2007 Sophie B retired from her job with the US Department of Energy in Washington, DC. She had been reluctant to leave work because she couldn't think what she'd do without it. She's taking time to adjust to her new situation:

> I am not yet comfortable being alone in my apartment. Often, I feel panic. I spend a lot of time trying to do at least one thing a day with a friend, which I see as impossible to keep up. When I am alone here, I am compulsive about phoning my friends and sons. My friends don't seem to mind having long conversations with me, but my two sons do!
>
> I eat many lunches and dinners alone at a place which is cheap and within walking distance, where I don't feel odd being alone. A lot of the folks who go there are also alone; on their computers, reading newspapers, looking out the windows, or people watching (my favourite pastime).

There are many lonely people living out their retirements who have little contact with others, and for whom freedom in this context has little meaning. Joan M, a community club member, says she notices that some single, older men who attend the club's weekly meetings and activities say they haven't spoken to anyone at all since the previous week's meeting. Another member, Annika R, further fills out the picture. She emigrated to Australia from The Netherlands in 1957 with her husband and two small children, retired in 1985, and has since met many older people through her work with organisations such as the Australian Health Department, the Department of Housing and Alzheimer's Australia. She comments:

> I have met elderly people living alone who are not lonely at all, but I also come across a lot of lonely people, lonely people living in retirement places, with lots of people around them. People whose first language is not English [Annika has a particular interest in migrants of Dutch origin] can be particularly isolated. Sometimes people in retirement places are avoided by other retirees for some reason or other, or they may have been duped by their own children or treated badly in some way that makes their lives a misery.

Misery of this kind is very disheartening and those who are able to alleviate some of the loneliness of people in this situation are doing something very worthwhile.

People who are married can be lonely and trapped within their marriages, but when there is happiness and companionship, to lose a partner can be a life-shattering experience. This kind of loss may make it temporarily impossible to sort out feelings of grief from feelings about the experience of living alone in retirement. Conrad D was a naval officer in the armed forces of The Netherlands until 1977, when he reached the compulsory retirement age of 50 and was given a 'replacement pension' until he turned 64, as was the custom. He says he never took a paid job after age discharge as: 'My dear wife liked me to stay with her, so I only worked a bit in politics and as a president of the council of an apartment building, both without pay'.

In 2003, Conrad's wife died, leaving him bereft. 'There remained only half of my life. My experience is that the fun, the love, the means to talk to someone have gone. For me there is not the slightest advantage in living alone. Only sorrow.' He now looks after the house and garden, including the repairs needed ('I am a 'do-it-yourselfer'), does clock repairs for friends, keeps up his social contacts to avoid becoming isolated, and is generally busy and usually short of time.

The ways people cope with the loss of a partner vary, but it is generally a struggle that involves determination and courage. Marilyn R, who worked in retail outlets in Sydney from the age of 15, lost her husband, George, previously a carpenter, about five years after they had retired jointly in 1998. They'd had a close marriage ('we always did everything together'), and enjoyed their retirement doing volunteering, visiting their grandchildren and their families, and spending their leisure time camping, fishing, prawning, going on picnics, and occasionally, as a treat, going to the live shows they both enjoyed.

Marilyn talks about the loneliness she experiences in spite of the fact that she makes every effort to be active and in touch with people. 'When George died I felt it would be so easy to pull up the bedclothes and not get up at all ever again', she admits. She recalls a definitive moment that helped her change direction: 'I found myself sitting bolt upright in bed thinking this isn't what George would have wanted for me'. Although Marilyn says she's come through the experience a much stronger and more independent person who can speak up for herself, she still grieves for George and lies awake for hours at night unable to sleep. She says her grandmother, who raised two children in difficult circumstances, remains an inspiration to her. 'When I think things are tough I know she had it tougher, yet she always had a smile for me.'

Marilyn works for Anglicare and the Starlight Foundation, provides transport for neighbours with disabilities, and is very involved in her craft activities. She initiates meeting up with old workmates 'so we can reminisce and have a laugh together'. Visitors, particularly family, are very welcome, and she made me feel at home immediately offering tea and homemade cakes at our interview in the kitchen of the home she and George had built together when they first married. According to Marilyn 'It's nice to set another place. It's better than the days when I laugh to myself about how lonely my knife and fork look there on the table.' She takes heart from her sons, saying their father would be proud of Marilyn and her new life. 'I'm on the right track and I've got to stay there,' she adds firmly.

Keeping busy with a non-profit business is helping Rosamund W deal with the difficulty and sadness of losing her husband, Ralph, in 2005. Rosamund's full-time career as a self-employed interior decorator in San Francisco was put on hold in the late 1990s when she spent a year in Rome with her husband and daughter. She did some volunteer work there in a cat sanctuary. She and her husband returned to Italy regularly after this, and in 2001 Rosamund's involvement with the cat sanctuary in Rome's historic centre, as well as her work with feral cats at her local humane society in San Francisco, led her to set up 'Friends of Roman Cats' as a non-profit organisation aiming to 'help Italy's stray cats [to] be spayed and neutered, and to spread the word in America of Italy's status as a no-kill country'.

She has phased out her decorating business and now only occasionally does some work for former clients, as so much time is taken up building her 'business'. As she explains:

> I very much like the mechanics of growing a business. I imagine I would have felt similar had I started this work earlier, but living alone has really made me focus more. I am lonely at times, as you would expect after 34 years of happy marriage, but I keep very busy between my animal work, art – I have been doing ceramics for 13 years and am now also doing watercolours – and friends. I suppose working with animals and growing a business, even one I make no money at, has helped keep me going emotionally.

Dealing with the facts

What else is of particular concern to people living alone? Is it difficult to know what to do with the time that becomes available to you once you retire? Do you worry about managing things on your own? Do women feel restricted about being out at night alone or travelling by themselves?

Most of the single people I talked with describe very full lives, and often complained of being afraid time will run out before they do all the things they want to do. Even so, some feel anxiety about how to fill in their days, especially if they've been involved in a high-powered job. Paul D retired from his position as a member of parliament in South Australia in 2006 at the age of 74. He says adapting to retirement has been reasonably easy, but there are some changes he's found difficult: 'Shifting from "being at the top of the pyramid", working in top gear when every minute is filled with a full staff waiting upon your direction, then suddenly becoming a "foot soldier" with time at your disposal certainly gives you pause for thought'.

Another aspect of retirement that he's noticing is the need to establish a different routine to his days. As an MP, Paul's life was very orderly. He'd get up at 6.17, for example ('yes, on the dot', he says – 'I had to ask!'), so as to be up and ready to catch the rural news, and from then until late in the evening he'd be fully occupied. Now he still rises at 6.17, but sometimes finds there are 'gaps of comparative boredom', usually from around 10.30 until 6. He doesn't want to join new things as that would make him feel 'locked in', and he already has enough meetings to attend with his ongoing political and environmental interests. Recently he's been invited to act for a campaign against the planting of genetically modified crops. He was pleased to be asked as he is committed to the cause and enjoys the work, but he doesn't see this as a long-term answer. Paul says he's considered going back to being a farmer – his place at Kangaroo Island could be used for this purpose, but he remains undecided about such a move. Divorced now for many years, he says he'll probably stay single and live alone, though he couldn't be said to be absolutely certain about that.

Filling in time haphazardly rather than using it to do what you really want to do is something that concerns Ceridwen C. She thinks she retired too early and that maybe she should have changed careers, even though her feelings towards the retired life, not necessarily the single life, are very positive. She says reflectively:

My retirement has been beset by too many doubts and failures, and not enough planning and value analysis. I find it is very easy to fritter time away. Without strong commitments the days drift by full of pleasant things and busy little tasks – you go to the library, the doctor, the service station, the supermarket; you arrange to have something repaired or maintained; you need a new telephone or fridge; you meet friends for coffee or lunch, do a little volunteer work, join a book group, go to a bridge club or a gym, join a Probus club, or just sit in the garden reading or doing crosswords. And there are always household tasks expanding and waiting to consume the day. And that's fine – but there may come a time when you wonder what you've been doing all these years.

I suppose what I think is that you need to get your

priorities right, to establish something you really want to do, whether it's to go and live by the sea, or make a garden, or write one's life story, or spend more time with grandchildren, or learn something completely new – but you mustn't let busyness prevent you. I have so many retired friends who want to do something, but are always saying 'But I'm just too busy'. It's a great excuse.

Many people find as they get older that physical limitations frustrate their ambitions to do things. Raymond K, the cost accountant, lives alone and is very fit, but he regrets that hand/eye coordination problems are affecting his golf. Playing and watching sport is something that's been important to him all his life, with cricket an obsession. 'I believe I know more about cricket records than anyone else in Australia.' In fact, he and a partner once won a jackpot worth £243 on *Give it a Go*, a radio program on 2GB hosted by the legendary Jack Davies, in the category of general sport. (To his relief, he says, the last question was a cricket question about Donald Bradman, though he credits his partner with being infinitesimally more sure about the answer than he was.) Raymond acknowledges he's always been competitive about sporting activity ('I used to get seriously depressed if we lost at cricket'), something most people prefer to keep a dark secret, but currently it is his golf game that is on his mind:

Other weaknesses don't worry me, but I have a severe weakness in my golf game – chipping and pitching. It's always been a weakness [he started playing at 15], but I've survived over the years as my long shots are fine. But now that I've lost some hand/eye coordination it's getting worse. My second son is a professional golfer and has taught me the mechanics so I know what I've got to do, but I can't do it. I think I get more frustrated than other people. I even went to a psychiatrist but it didn't help.

There are, of course, many people with far more serious physical problems, as Raymond would be the first to acknowledge. Living alone may not make that much difference to how you feel, but then again it may be that problems loom larger when there's no one on hand with whom to talk things over. It's hard to say.

When there are important decisions to be made, people who live alone are usually obliged to take sole responsibility and to live with the consequences. This isn't necessarily a disadvantage. As Cecily B, a former secretary and then part-time shorthand typist for a doctor in London, who retired in 2002, explains: 'Being alone [her husband died in 1990] and retired can make one more confident, depending on your disposition. For me, it has made me very independent, knowing that I alone must bear the consequences of any action I take.' Cecily, who is in her mid-eighties, likes to let the housework wait 'while I go out discovering London on my own'. She also flies to Bergerac in the Dordogne three times a year to visit her daughter and husband, something her husband would not have done, as he would never fly. According to Cecily, her old school motto, translated from the Latin, 'He conquers who conquers himself', is 'most appropriate for people like me'.

About half of the singles I interviewed are on some kind of pension. Some express regret about not having given more thought to their financial futures. Ceridwen C, for example, says she found herself so busy with immediate demands that she hadn't got around to making longer term financial plans:

I deeply regret that I did not look into my finances more responsibly. I was only 56 when I retired, and there was a long way to go. I keep telling myself that money will not make me happy – but it would make life more enjoyable and secure. To travel in comfort (my car is fourteen years old and falling apart); to buy some nice clothes; to take up subscriptions to opera, theatre and concerts; to give to my children; to have private medical insurance and a house cleaner; to have the house painted and refurbished; to add beauty to my environment – yes, all that would be very nice

– but it wouldn't help with the big questions, and I'd still be my perverse, yearning self.

Others who find themselves in lower income brackets say they organise their lives by making careful choices about using the money they do have. As Leila J explains:

> I regret the drop in income, but find there are so many things that can be done for very little cost such as art galleries and museums. I am wholeheartedly appreciative of the cheap public transport available for older people. For instance, I have just been with a walking group going from Coalcliff to Austinmer, NSW, which included walking across the fantastic Sea Cliff Bridge. Travel there and back, using buses and trains, cost me a whole $2.50! What greater bargain could possibly be found. We took our lunches so the only other cost for a great day out was for a cup of coffee before we caught the train to return home.

Over the span of a career, women are generally paid less than men, and may also have been out of the workforce for many years with family responsibilities. Diana Olsberg, a researcher in the field of the sociology of ageing, tells me single women are more at risk of poverty in old age than men. Speculation about baby boomers' finances in retirement suggests the majority of those who will be poor or near poor will be singles, especially single women.

Married people have each other when they are ill, and

companionship on tap, but single people don't have this kind of support readily available. Many single people mention health problems or operations – loss of sight or hearing, knee surgery, heart surgery and so on – and may mention a sister's or brother's help or that of a friend, but reference to their being without support is not a common complaint. And yet it must be of great concern sometimes. I think of occasions when I've been incapacitated and unable to get out of bed and wondered what I would do if there were no one there to look after me. Perhaps people used to living alone become very resourceful in these situations. I found Leila J's way of talking about her health problems typical of the attitude of most single people – they don't go into detail (at least in an interview situation) and they often take a positive attitude:

I have had two hip replacements and know what it is to be much less mobile than I am now, so these days I work at maintaining fitness and mobility. I have membership at a 'centre for healthy ageing', where I do exercise classes and gym sessions. I also walk with a walking group one morning each week.

I also recall a conversation with Ernestine M, who is close to 80, that lifted my spirits. 'How are you, Ernestine?' I asked. 'Very well, thank you', she replied cheerfully. 'In fact, I seem to get healthier the older I get!'

In many cases financial and health concerns for those living alone would undoubtedly be more serious than is evident from these conversations. Yet people have a remarkable capacity to rise above the factual realities of their existence. The life of the mind and of the imagination is often seen as an equally, or more, important consideration. Many people find themselves looking ahead to what they can achieve and do, rather than focusing on what they are not able to do.

Travelling alone can have particular drawbacks for single people. Many see it as grossly unfair that a supplement is incurred for single accommodation. Those who would like to travel with a companion often find it hard to locate someone who is suitable and available. As Peggy D says: 'I would like to have single friends who want to travel. It's not much fun going alone as a Party of One!' Travelling in a group may not suit, and for women it has long been thought unwise to travel alone, particularly at night.

Yet travelling far and wide is what many single people do – men and women, sometimes alone though more often in groups. Single travelling seems to be booming in ways it never has in the past. The Travel Industry Association in the United States reports that in the three years between

2004 and 2007 almost 25 per cent of adults took a solo vacation, and that the baby boomer contingent has the highest travel volume of any age group. Websites are proliferating, with names such as 'Gutsy Women Travel' and 'Adventure Women', to offer support for women who want to travel together. Community clubs of various kinds also provide opportunities for travelling in groups and many singles report on the success of these.

It is not unusual for women or men to travel alone in camper vans and other forms of transport, and to enjoy themselves immensely. Leila J, for example, loves to travel:

> At 64 it was time to do some of the travelling I'd wanted to do while I was still fit and well. The first year I spent a month in the Philippines, then bought a Toyota HiAce camper van and spent six months on the road, travelling through Western Australia, Northern Territory, South Australia, Victoria and Tasmania. Since then I have been back to many of these places, especially Victoria, where most of my family are and where all my grandchildren live.

Since retirement Leila has also travelled to Canada, Thailand, Egypt, Greece, Italy and several African countries such as Kenya, Tanzania, Zimbabwe and South Africa, which included a three-week tour from Capetown ending at Victoria Falls in Zambia. She adds:

> I like company, but when you live by yourself you are used to doing things by yourself and I pretty much take it for

granted. I have given some thought about joining a safari-style trip with other solo travellers (they are on offer from time to time with the campervan and motor-home club I belong to), but have so far not done so. I am seriously thinking of next year travelling to Turkey, Spain and Scotland, and seeing some of the parts of New South Wales that have previously been bypassed because they are closer to home.

Adventure and travel, it seems, are alive and well in the hearts of intrepid singles.

Lone ranging

Many single people are involved in life 'up to the chin' to borrow a phrase Bernard Shaw used to describe his own extraordinary life ('up to the chin in the life of my own time'). A catalogue of activities engaged in by some singles suggests there wouldn't be much time left over for loneliness. Ellie P is involved in a wide range of projects, travel and other activities that leave her with barely a minute to spare: 'I do try to stay at home to watch *Landline* on Sundays', she says nonchalantly.

Ellie began her retirement by doing a three-month government-sponsored training course in cooking during the Sydney Olympics. She says she met an incredible range of people from all walks of life, people she'd barely realised existed when she was 'cloistered' by her narrow working life. 'This got me interested and moving – I was out everyday and I got my confidence back.' Ellie joined a Probus club with a friend and volunteered to organise their monthly tours, an exhausting and demanding job that she 'ran like clockwork' for three years. When she realised men were being given priority on the waiting list, she decided to give up this voluntary work. The practice offended her: 'I asked if the club was an ageing marriage market. They ignored my complaints. I decided it was time to go.'

Some of the highlights of her other activities include being a volunteer at a hospital being built in Kathmandu and trekking in Nepal; doing volunteer work in remote areas in Australia where she stayed six weeks at a time at different properties to help students doing education by correspondence; joining the University of the Third Age (this took her to Prague on an exchange program and she regularly billets people visiting Australia in return); travelling to Turkey alone and to China with a group; travelling to Burma to give advice on whether an artist's work would be marketable in Australia ('I've got the eye. They know I can tell who is up and coming'); walking an hour a day, regular bushwalking and canoeing. She learned the latter skill at a council program for seniors, where she was taught by an ex-convict from Maitland jail. 'He took out his glass eye for us – it was marvellous!' she recalls.

Ellie's philosophy is that you can't sit around like Cinderella. What she likes most about the single life in retirement is having more time for friends, being able to mix widely in a way she never could in her working life, and not having to please anyone. She now sees the city from a different angle and finds women drink and socialise far more than they used to do. She says she has many loving, platonic and other relationships, and prefers this to 'a crowded life of regular contact' with family members. Two future goals are of interest to her: buying a one-person canoe so she can poke around places like Lake George near Canberra when bushwalking becomes too difficult, and joining the euthanasia society so she can 'go out with dignity'.

An interesting dimension of Ellie's story that doesn't emerge in this account is the role of art in her life. Indeed, the first things I noticed when I arrived at Ellie's home for our interview were the colourful paintings, some seeming to bring the garden right into the room, others more abstract but vibrant and lively. 'Art has always sustained me', she explains. She studied art for the Higher School Certificate in 1959, but doesn't recall Australian art being part of that course. When married and living in Canberra, she went to see Leonard French's 'Seven Days of Creation' exhibition, which she describes as 'simply the most magnificent thing I'd ever seen. It was a tragedy that the series was later dispersed.' This experience launched her on gallery visiting – she'd put her son and pusher in her Morris Minor and set off to galleries wherever she was living. 'Art was my lifeblood through all my difficult times', she acknowledges. I wonder how true this is for others. To what extent, and in what ways do art, music and literature make the experience of being human more bearable, more joyous? Are the humanities the unsung heroes that offer hope, solace and inspiration for us in the face of life's limitations? I'd like to think so.

Another lone ranger with a life chock full of activity is Clive G who spent 44 years with the Sydney County Council (now Energy Australia), beginning as an apprentice fitter and turner and becoming an engineer draftsman. He retired in 1982 at the age of 60, and spent the last 14 years of his wife's life as her carer. 'I was housebroke by the time she died in 1998', Clive muses ruefully. He has been on a blind pension for the last 16 years. 'I look on losing my sight as a challenge. It happened fairly suddenly as a result of macular degeneration. Vision Australia provides me with lots of help.'

Clive's life is extraordinarily busy. In fact, it took several attempts for me to fit in an interview with him as his weeks were so tightly booked. Even when I finally pinned him down we had to change our arrangements because his next-door neighbour had been burgled and his carpentry skills were called upon to mend the lock on her door! Clive has been involved with volunteering in many different ways, including helping out at a toy repair group that delivers toys to those in need, and providing support and encouragement for peer groups at Vision Australia. He also developed a gadget that helps visually impaired people to cut timber straight, and he trains 'blind' people in the use of it to help improve their timber cutting. And he has his family responsibilities – two children, four grandchildren and seven great grandchildren. 'I love every one of them', he says.

He attends classes of all kinds – Australian history and the history of the Sydney Harbour Bridge have been recent favourites; he attends a community club and goes on all their outings (he'd just returned from a successful five-day trip to Bateman's Bay); and he attends church regularly. He attends a discussion group with a local school for seniors where he likes to listen to their choir. 'I always loved singing but I'm a bit deaf now, so I don't sing in it.' He also plays lawn bowls, 'although I can't really see the jack', he laughs. After all these events he always has a meal with the members of the various organisations to which he belongs. Eating out means he can manage living at home more easily. 'Of course, I can't see the dust', he says, 'but an old family friend helps me out with that'. His only real complaint is that 'things that used to take me five minutes now take 45 minutes'. Clive's positive approach to life and his pleasure in people and activities are admirable. But it is his taking part so cheerfully in lawn bowls that really impressed me. What a spirit!

~

Attitudes towards singles have undergone a profound change, and so has their social and economic status. Most people who live alone seem to enjoy their lives and become wedded to the freedoms it entails. This is true even for those who initially are apprehensive or dread the experience, as more often than not it seems to turn out better than expected.

Living alone involves less loneliness than you might anticipate, and many single people have lives full to the brim with multiple activities. Some yearn for a partner, but many think they have become too settled in their ways, too 'selfish' and enjoying of their freedom, to take on a live in relationship. Keeping 'in charge of the silence', rather than having the silence in charge of you is something most who 'go it alone' appear to have well in hand.

Whether you live alone or with a partner, when you retire you often reconsider where you want to live. Some may have always longed to live by the water, or in the bush or the mountains, and they think now is the time to make the move. Others want to be in the heart of things and so choose to move closer to a city centre. Some decide they don't want to move at all. In the next chapter we meet people who have dealt with these dilemmas and track the implications of their various choices.

Sea changes,
tree changes and
other options

Two voices are there; one is of the sea,
One of the mountains; each a mighty voice

Wordsworth, 1807

Many voices, all beckoning in different directions, are apt to call when people are deciding where to live in retirement: the sea, the mountains, the city, the country, the seaside, safe old suburbia, or some other way of life altogether. Robert Browning describes the human mind caught up in the contradictions of just such a dilemma in his poem, published in 1855, 'Up at a villa – Down in the city', that recalls a time early in his marriage to Elizabeth Barrett Browning when they were staying in a villa outside the city of Siena, Italy. Throughout the poem the narrator rails at the disadvantages of living in the city – 'fowls, wine, at double the rate', deciding 'And so, the villa for me, not the city!' But then memories of the excitement of city life overwhelm him and his mind is changed again: 'Oh, a day in the city-square, there is no such pleasure in life!'

Questions as to whether or not to move house, and *where* to move if the decision gets the thumbs up, are of concern to most retired people. Decisions on the subject have particular poignancy at this stage of life: people are conscious they are preparing for a different kind of future, and possibly one when they'll be less able to do some of the things they can do now. To move house at any stage has serious financial implications, even more so in retirement.

For most people, retirement means not joining the traffic in the peak hour every day. This removes a restriction that may have prevented them moving house earlier. For some, downsizing is part of their financial plan; others may be keen to pursue a different lifestyle or to move closer to family members; others choose to live somewhere that is easier to manage, or enables them to lockup and leave so they can travel; and others decide they don't want to move at all.

The location you choose determines who you are able to spend your everyday time with, and what activities or pursuits will be readily available to you. I envy my sister-in-law, for example, who lives in Melbourne near a tram that takes seven minutes to reach the art gallery where she is a volunteer guide. I love going to the art gallery in Sydney, but it takes me so long to get there and back that I mostly only make it to the major exhibitions, and volunteering is out of the question, given all the other things I want to fit into my life. Yet when I weigh up this disadvantage against other advantages related to where I live, I decide the inner city life is not for me. Fortunately, my husband is of a similar opinion. If partners are at odds about a decision of this kind then you have to rely on compromises, and sometimes major compromises, to resolve those differences.

There are many factors to be weighed up and taken into account when deciding where, when, how and if to move. Factors that may occur in the future and about which you can only hazard a guess also need to be thought about. If you are part of a couple and one of you were to die, would the remaining partner be happy in the new community? If you move to live close to family or friends will you be content in your new place of residence if they move? If your decision to move is based on enabling you to deep sea fish or play golf or follow some other physical activity more easily, and your health fails, will you regret your decision?

In spite of all these complexities many people do change location and adopt different lifestyles soon after retiring. What, then, propels people to make the decision to move or not to move house, what kinds of moves do they tend to make, and what sort of issues emerge from the process?

Sea changes

The house name 'Wyewurk' at Thirroul Beach on the south coast of NSW, where D. H. Lawrence wrote some of his novel *Kangaroo* in 1920, represents Australian humour on the subject of life beside the sea at its laconic best. Many retirement advertisements pick up on the dream of an idyllic stress-free life beside the sea featuring technicolour beach scenes of happy couples wandering hand in hand with nothing to do but enjoy themselves. To live beside the water can represent a dream come true, but like any other change of this nature it won't necessarily be problem free, even if the problems are relatively insignificant in the grander scheme of things.

A couple planning to move to a seaside destination already made familiar from regular holidays, a couple who have made a successful move to Lake Macquarie on the coast of New South Wales, and a couple who have moved from rural New South Wales to a coastal area in Brisbane, but remain undecided about whether they have made the right choice, tell their stories below.

The seaside retirement plans of Leah E, a former flight attendant and more recently a remedial massage therapist in Sydney, illustrate the problems that can arise in planning to turn dreams of idyllic retirement by the sea into reality. Leah explains that when she retires with her husband to a home in the seaside community with golfing facilities on the south coast of New South Wales where they now regularly holiday, the irony is that they may well need to find a bigger house than they currently have. If she is to continue with occasional remedial massage, even if just for friends and family, she'll need a treatment room, and both she and her husband would like to have office and computer space – something they don't have at present. They'll also need space to house the children and grandchildren when they visit. One of their children is moving overseas and that makes it even more important to have room for the family to stay.

According to Leah these are problems faced by many other retired friends who are now living in this popular seaside community. She points out that it is hard to plan how to buy a house that will accommodate the new lifestyle you think you'll have with the limited resources of retirement. They hope their children will visit, but will they? They think they'll need more space for their personal interests but who can really tell?

She has seen some people rattling around in large houses that they thought they'd need and find they never use, and others not having provided nearly enough room for comfortable living, particularly when the family arrives to enjoy their holidays. There is a difficult balancing act necessary between trying to make a wise financial decision in relation to the type and size of house you purchase, and ensuring your housing is suitable for your needs as they unfold.

~

For Russell P, and his wife Tanya, the move to living on the water has been a great success. Russell, a high school deputy, retired when he was 58 at the end of 1993, after he'd achieved all he'd hoped for in his career and was finding the job repetitious; while his wife, Tanya, a social sciences head teacher, retired at the age of 60 in 2001. She feared that the pace and workload of her position – she was working around 70 hours a week – would shorten her life.

They both phased into retirement with some part-time work, but once fully retired they were delighted with their decision: 'Once I had "let go" I found retirement just wonderful. The freedom to do whatever I pleased was better than any previous holiday, when the shadow of getting organised for the next term was ever present', Tanya recalls. They'd long had plans to retire somewhere near the water. Tanya describes their search:

> We'd always fancied having a waterfront (doesn't everyone?), but it was beyond our means. When driving back to Sydney from Newcastle in January 1995, we turned off at the Bonnell's Bay sign and drove around the area of southern Lake Macquarie [a large saltwater lake on the coast of New South Wales], writing down a few phone numbers from the FOR SALE signs.
>
> We were hoping to find a block of land on the water, perhaps with a cabin or boatshed on it, and planned to put our caravan there for use as a weekend retreat. As it

turned out, the last place we looked at was a full house, with a flat underneath, just the right height above the water, on a waterfront reserve, with an easterly aspect across the lake. Russell said 'This is it!' And it was.

They bought the house, rented it out for two years, and then Russell began to refurbish it. 'I'd drive up every Wednesday and do a couple of days' work, mostly tidying up and painting, and Tanya would take the train up on Friday afternoon and we'd stay for the weekend, driving back to our Sydney townhouse on Sunday nights.' They now spend about 95 per cent of their time at the lake walking, swimming and gardening on their three-quarter acre lot, following various hobbies and regularly visiting Newcastle and Sydney for social occasions and babysitting duties. They still do a few weeks of 'work' [supervising university examinations] a year. 'It's about as much as we feel like doing in the way of paid work', Russell admits.

How do they feel about their decision to move to the lake? According to Russell, 'I love being able to commune with the environment – there are great sunrises and sunsets up here – being away from the city, and being surrounded by peace and quiet'. He votes it a success. Tanya says they've never regretted their decision:

It has worked out wonderfully well. We had the luxury of being able to acclimatise gradually to living out of the city. We are very lucky to still have our place in Sydney [currently a son is living there with his family] we can use when we visit. It is important to me, as my elderly parents are in Sydney and I like to visit them every week. While I did love teaching, I just adore being retired – every day is Saturday!

They give themselves another ten years at the lake when Russell will be 80 and Tanya aged 75. They think then, or maybe even before, they may not be able to maintain things 'as we'd want them to be'. At some stage they might consider buying into a retirement village.

The fact that the sea change has worked out well for Russell and Tanya may have a lot to do with the gradual way they made the transition and their retaining a bolthole in the city. Not everyone is able to manage this, and some don't even want to do so, but for others it may be a key factor for success.

~

Until retiring in 2006, Anne and Alan C lived and worked on 26 hectares of land in rural New South Wales in the Hawkesbury area, growing and selling cut flowers, a physically demanding, seven-day-a-week affair. Anne modestly describes herself as also being 'a local artist of sorts'. Alan had worked on their property for 35 years, but when he reached 70 and was having some difficult health problems they decided 'it was time to retire'. Once the decision was made they both really looked forward to their retirement, though it took them another 15 months to sell their property.

Staying in their home wasn't a good option because of the extremes of climate, the costly upkeep, and the need to use the capital to fund their retirement. A priority for Alan was to be near medical resources so they weren't necessarily thinking of a sea change at that stage. Adelaide, Newcastle and Brisbane were considered because of various connections they had with these places. Finding somewhere suitable while still running the business was difficult. Eventually, using the Internet, Alan found a place in Brisbane that was near the sea:

> We'd previously been introduced to the Redland Bay area when visiting Brisbane for family holidays, and by a flower grower we met through our business, and we knew we loved it there. We would not have considered living in any other part of Brisbane, especially anywhere without a sea breeze. Having lived where we had for over 30 years had made us yearn for a cool breeze.

They were a little apprehensive about the decision but, as Alan explains, they thought they'd be able to overcome any problems:

> We have a son and grandchildren living in Brisbane, and even knowing that it's usually not a good idea to follow your children, and knowing that the grandchildren were teenagers with their own lives, we thought it would work out.
>
> Anne did not see the house prior to purchase but

there was something about it that I knew she would like. It was on one level with a reasonably sized garden and was a bit different from the usual. We would have preferred to build an environmentally sensitive and energy efficient home, but that was beyond our means.

Has the move worked out well? 'Yes and no', says Alan. 'On the whole, I suppose it hasn't', counters Anne. She adds:

We love the house, the area and the climate. We love our walks to the sea and all that goes with it – birds, mangroves and so on, and to have that close by and within walking distance is very important to us. The places we've explored are beautiful. Our son is sometimes glad we've come up here, and sometimes not, but he didn't think it was the right move for us in the first place. Our grandchildren are always glad to see us, but we don't see them a lot.

I have a project of painting all of the flowers in our garden as they come out, which I find absorbing. But Alan feels he hasn't much purpose here and that worries us. The obvious thing is to join groups, but joining groups later in life isn't easy, and it doesn't necessarily mean you'll make friends. I joined a local art society, which was a good move. Yet some people in my group don't even seem to remember my name after my being with them once a week for eight months!

Alan says he is finding it difficult to adjust to being retired. They don't do the gardening they imagined they'd do, mainly because of the drought, and neither is he following up on his other plans:

> I've had a lot of trouble coping with the sense that everything is over and that I really no longer have any purpose. Anne doesn't seem to worry about having a purpose; she has her art, and she is much more outgoing and able to make friends than I am. I have on the other hand not developed any outside interests and I have, if I ever had any, few socialising skills.
>
> I also find that although I had good intentions of joining and doing things like land care and photography, when it came to it I didn't want to spend my days pulling out weeds in messy, weed-infested swamps, and photography today is spend, spend, spend! We enjoy occasional day trips to the Glass Mountains, Bribie Island, Tambourine and so on. And camping trips are something we are thinking about.

It is still early days as it is less than a year since Anne and Alan moved. Retiring from a working life that was all-consuming, having Alan's ongoing health difficulties that have proved costly and prevented some retirement options, and leaving behind all that was known and familiar to move interstate is a heady combination. They are certainly reluctant to move again. Anne says they are conscious of how lucky they really are, but that doesn't make the adjustment process any easier.

Tree changes

A move to the mountains from the suburbs was the choice made by three of the couples I interviewed. Their stories illustrate the pleasures and the pitfalls that can accompany such a choice. The first couple thinks it was probably worthwhile, though they are not absolutely sure; the second have only minor reservations about their new lifestyle; while the third tried the experiment, found it wanting, and returned to their former home.

Geoff P's decision to retire from his work with the British army where he had served for 30 years before joining the Ministry of Defence as a civil servant was influenced by his wife Avril inheriting half of her family's home in Llangollen, Wales, after her mother's death in 2006. Very little beyond what was necessary for survival had been done to the house or the garden for around 15 years, so when they decided to move there they had a major restoration project on their hands. Geoff explains the background to their decision:

As an 'army brat' I had very few geographical roots, and then I joined the army myself. Avril and I lived in army quarters until 1998 when we bought a house about 35 miles west of London. This was largely to keep on the property ladder rather than as a retirement place. Apart from a break of two and a half years we lived in that house until I finally left the army.

Neither of us liked the frenetic and crowded life of

southeast England and when I retired Avril wanted to move back to Wales. We decided to buy Avril's sister's share of the house their mother had left them. The house was not what we planned, as we felt it too large to be comfortable, but it is in a very good location with wonderful views, and there was nothing remotely comparable available elsewhere in the town.

The nomadic life of the army makes any regular career for wives difficult. Avril did voluntary work wherever she was in temporary residence, and her most recent casual job was a two-year stint as a postwoman near their south London home. Geoff's retirement enabled their decision to move to Wales, a decision he was 'a hundred per cent behind'. But it had special meaning for Avril, as inheriting a share of her family home made it possible for her to return to a community with whom she had strong connections and to the beloved Welsh hills of her childhood.

The renovations needed to the house were extensive and, according to Geoff, involved many more problems than they'd anticipated:

> The house was/is a challenge. Mother-in-law was an avid shopper and never threw anything away, and was also inclined towards the belief that money spent on maintenance was wasted, a view exacerbated when she had to live on a widow's pension. The house was crammed full of her possessions, and the garage contained, among other things, five defunct large upright freezers full of teaching

notes and exam papers covering 40 years. We also had to cram in a houseful of our own furniture.

Trying to dispose of items became a source of friction as Avril and I both have differing priorities, as do our children and relatives. We find ourselves acting as a warehouse for 'prized' possessions of others, but not 'prized' enough for them to clutter their own homes!

With redecorating and the general state of flux, things would go missing, providing another cause for irritation. Additional difficulties included the continual presence of workmen, the scaffolding, much moving of heavy furniture, the smell of paint and noise of hammers and drills, wintry conditions, setbacks with plumbing and drains, endless decision-making, trips to bleak DIY establishments, and, above all, the endless clutter. Another anxiety was that for the first time in their lives they were tending to spend more than they earned, and as their earnings were significantly reduced, Geoff found this 'slightly scary'.

They were also now both at home together full time. Avril had not anticipated this would be a problem, but the situation brought out their differences and at times things have been less harmonious than usual:

The problem is we approach impasses very differently and our priorities often don't coincide. On so many occasions we pulled apart instead of together. I think I wanted a 'quick fix' solution so that we could rapidly return to our normal peaceful existence and enjoy retirement before it was too late. Geoff, on the other hand, sensibly wanted a permanent solution, as he would mainly be responsible for maintenance.

Visits from family and friends are welcomed by both: it gives them a rest from their 'Grand Project' and they take the time to appreciate the countryside surrounding them – one of the main reasons they moved there. Geoff is learning field botany from a new friend, an environmental consultant, and helps him with his surveys monitoring cliff nesting birds. Geoff is a bit wary of joining new clubs as 'it takes time to earn your credentials'.

Avril has thought a lot about the effects of the move on their relationship:

I don't think either of us appreciated how very difficult it would be. Subsequently, although I have regretted my frequent outbursts of anger and hated the tension created almost daily at the worst times, I have never, unlike Geoff, been moved to say very bitterly, 'I wish we had never moved'.

It worried me that Geoff sometimes really meant his words of regret. Fortunately, we seem to have worked through most of the difficulties and now that the major steps in renovation have been executed, I can almost enjoy analysing the possible reasons for how stressful it has all been.

This will not be their last move. They have bought a flat 'for when we become infirm', as they realise their present house will be unmanageable under those conditions. However, for the present, Avril views their experiences philosophically:

> The fact that friends and family feel that our new home is worth visiting, even in its unfinished condition, proves that the venture has been a good move. Inheriting half a house and selling our own property fairly easily at least obviated financial problems and somehow we seem to have survived the upheaval, but I should not like to take the risk again.

Kelly and Simon M retired together in 2001, a process that 'involved a bit of juggling'. Simon had enjoyed a staged retirement process, stepping down from senior roles in civil engineering/building management to work on projects for the NSW Government Royal Commission into the Building industry. His final contractual position, which involved desktop publishing and 'full-on photo journalism', allowed him to work from home. His wife, Kelly, after bringing up their four children, began a late career as a French and English teacher, becoming very involved in school life and extra-curricular activities.

They'd planned to sell the family home they'd lived in for 25 years and to downsize to somewhere different, as this would give them capital to add to their allocated pensions. It all happened more quickly than they expected. Their house sold the day they put it on the market and they found themselves in a new home in the Blue Mountains just five months after leaving full-time work – 'a huge change to adjust to since so much happened all at once' according to Kelly, though Simon felt he made the adjustment 'within a few weeks'.

The Blue Mountains 'won' the location wars because of its cool climate, the big range of activities on offer, its beauty, and its distinctive identity and World Heritage listing. Kelly was in favour of it because of its proximity to Sydney, and while three of their children live overseas they 'all call Sydney home'. They both knew the area well; Simon, in particular, knew it 'intimately' as a weekend bushwalker, horse rider, abseiler, bike rider, 'canyoner' and camper.

The first step was to complete minor renovations (on a much smaller scale than that undertaken by Geoff and Avril) and to add more native plants to their garden. Their son, who has always lived in apartments, offered helpful advice: 'Get used to multipurpose rooms now you are in a smaller house'. As a result, Kelly designed a wall of desk/

storage/display units for their living room, which has given her a place to do her writing.

They joined everything (a book club, a French language discussion group, a philosophy forum, a walking group, the golf club, a tennis club) and Simon took on committee roles, including that of publications officer with the Blue Mountains Conservation Society. Both volunteered their services for bush care work in their local Jamison Creek catchment area, and Simon 'began mountain biking the roads and fire trails in a big way'. They make regular trips to Sydney to go to concerts and plays, and sometimes to visit their Sydney doctor and dentist who they haven't yet relinquished. They also have broadband and two new PCs. 'Couples need mutual space and independence – and two cars, separate offices, computers and email addresses are a big help', according to Simon.

It is now a few years since they moved to the mountains. How has it all worked out for them? Kelly's feelings were a little ambivalent to begin with:

I experienced a period of mourning for friends and family in Sydney, and a sense of loss of my readymade and actual circle of friends at school, and also a (smaller) sense of loss of identity as a teacher, even though I was ready to retire from work. I suppose I was a bit angry at Simon because we'd moved, even though the reasons were very logical, and I'd been very much part of the process. But time is making a difference and I'm beginning to feel well settled.

Simon attributes the success of their move to long and careful planning, and 'a little bit of bloomin' luck'. He is pleased that so far things have gone smoothly:

> Our marital relationship in retirement is as close and loving as ever, and even more serene. We do things together, but also follow individual pursuits. I am a great 'mover-on' and our appointment books have taken on a major importance. There are so many more entries that can be made when one does not have to block out five days a week!

The Blue Mountains was also the destination chosen by Sally and Harry O when they decided to move there during their retirement. They had emigrated from South Africa to Australia with their four children in 1968. Sally's background is in psychology, statistics and computer science. She worked full time for the health department in New South Wales until her retirement in 1994. She then completed a PhD on the effects of ear, throat and nose surgery in young children, graduating in 2005. From time to time she has worked casually as a research assistant helping university staff with statistical research related to various projects.

Harry had retired in 1988, before Sally, from his job as an internal assessment manager for a multinational business organisation. After doing maintenance and gardening jobs around the home, he found himself 'doing nothing' – he didn't like the feeling. As a result, he trained as a driving instructor, and according to Sally he 'became a legend' in this role. It satisfied his love of contact with people, something he'd felt he was missing out on when he'd retired the first time. After leaving this second job, Harry invested in buying rental property, including a house in Katoomba.

It was in 2002 that Sally and Harry decided to move to the Katoomba property. Their cash flow was not working out as they'd hoped, and a bout of pneumonia for Harry was making his chronic asthma quite debilitating. Unusually, when Harry was camping at the Katoomba house in freezing, rainy conditions, working to improve the property for letting, he was suddenly much freer of his asthma. This fact, and the realisation that they'd get a better rental return on their suburban home, led to their deciding to try out life in the mountains.

Sally supported the idea of moving in the hope it would be helpful for Harry's health, but at the same time she didn't really want to live in the mountains. 'I was reluctant from the start. In fact, deep down I was really angry about it and felt it was Harry's fault we had to do this.'

They settled into their new home with Harry enjoying the tasks of home improvement and looking after the large garden. They were about three kilometres from the village and planned to join local groups or classes but somehow found they never had the time.

Sally had many reasons for returning regularly to Sydney. She liked to touch base with her university work, to maintain links with family, including babysitting their grandchildren, keeping up with friends (for example, she'd been part of a group doing adult education courses each year since 1969), and attending her regular Saturday ballet classes with her daughter, followed by their having coffee together, a long established ritual.

Travelling backwards and forwards so frequently was tiring and she particularly disliked returning to the mountains at night. 'I felt guilty when I left Harry alone, especially when I stayed in Sydney overnight. He did feel a sense of isolation when I was away, though he understood my need to be there.' When Harry, too, found himself coming to Sydney three times a week over a six-month period for intensive chiropractic sessions, he came to understand that they just lived too far away. As Sally said: 'Harry's Sydney visits turned the tide and we decided to move back to our home in Hornsby'.

When I met with Sally (and her granddaughter, Daisy, whom she was minding that day) at a local coffee shop, she and Harry had barely settled back. They were both very pleased to be 'home' again, though they were dismayed at how much everything was costing – moving a second time, the renovations that were now needed, and all the extra expenses. As Sally says, 'It is a furphy that you need less money when you are retired. You need more. You want to do so many more things!'

Harry, as well as working on the renovations and the garden, is now working up his skills as a pianist, and hoping for a better run of health. Sally doesn't have to travel so far for her ballet lessons, and they are both glad the experiment is over.

Down in the city

Moves closer to the city have advantages to offer that many retired people are keen to enjoy. When Sophie B left her job in Washington, DC, feeling highly apprehensive about her future, she decided to move from her condominium in a small building to one in a larger building located in a more urbanised area. She says that even though she finds being alone in her apartment uncomfortable at times, the move itself has been good for her:

> The new building is full of friendly retired people and I already know about ten, mostly widows, to hang out with, although they are somewhat older than I am (which makes me feel older, too). The other pluses of my move are: I am within walking distance of our metro system, a grocery store, a community centre, and offices and medical buildings. My building is not a retirement community, it just sounds (and acts) like one.

Moving closer to the heart of things has made it easier for Sophie to find things to do, including going to 'lots and lots of movies with various friends', taking courses at a nearby learning institute sponsored by American University, and volunteering her services one afternoon a week reading for the blind and dyslexic.

City life has also been the choice of Hugo D and his wife. Although Hugo retired a few years back, his wife, a school principal of a city school, is not thinking of retiring. For a time they alternated between spending weekdays in a small apartment in the city, and weekends in their suburban home, about a 35-minute drive away. After several years, the travel in increasingly busy Sydney traffic became a strong disincentive for this choice of lifestyle, and they decided to join two apartments together to extend their city home and live in the city full time.

Hugo recognises that the decision to sell their suburban home brought some serious changes: 'For example, running in Ku-Ring-Gai Chase park was really important to me. I liked the trees, the silence. Hyde Park is not silent and the trees are not the same. It's not that I'm not looking forward to life in the city, but it will certainly be different.'

When I spoke to him again more recently about their move, and referred to his regrets about leaving the trees behind, he barely recalled having had those feelings. He is well adapted to city life now and enjoys eating out, attending the opera, and being in touch with all that is happening. Their out-of-city time is provided for with well-planned holidays that offer plenty of sea and tree changes.

The open road

Other lifestyle options adopted by people after they retire include living in a 'home' that travels with you to wherever you choose, or staying put in the home you were in before you retired. Living part (or even all) of the time travelling in a caravan, campervan, motor home or other similar form of transport involves a radical change of lifestyle. Australians call people who follow this path 'grey nomads', while in Canada and the United States the term 'RVers' (recreational vehicle travellers) is used, and those who travel long distances to winter in warmer climates are known as 'snowbirds'. On the dashboards of these vehicles you sometimes find clocks that cock a snook at time – measuring it by days instead of hours, or with numbers scattered randomly over the clock face above the words 'Who cares?', a touch of humour not unlike that in the name choice of 'Wyewurk' for a beachside cottage.

In Australia about 350 000 grey nomads are said to be 'roaming the country's highways and backroads' (*Sydney Morning Herald*, April 2007). Many of them do the 'Big Lap', a rite of passage that involves circumnavigating the country by road; others wander where and when they will within Australia; while others choose overseas countries for their travels, or a mixture of both.

A less radical form of 'nomadding' involves taking a biking tour. Jim Millar, previously a detective superintendent, spends his new life, now that he is retired, as a part-time biking tour guide in New Zealand. In an article titled 'Seniors reborn on their bikes' (*The Press*, 21 January 2008) Millar claims: 'It's the participation and sociability of the activity that draws most of the people ... most clients have reached a stage in their life when they want to maximise their enjoyment from life and to extend themselves while they are still able.'

Grey nomadding in its various disguises is currently a popular subject of media reports. A growing number of blogs are also being used to communicate the adventures of these travellers, and as the proportion of people over 65 in many countries increases, it seems that even greater numbers will hit the roads in the days to come. The nomadding experiences of two couples, Sarah and Craig A, and Angela and Brad M, in a motor home and caravan respectively, are described below.

Sarah and Craig A spend long stretches of time, from six months to two years, motor homing in Australia and Europe, particularly in France and Spain. Sarah's parents provided the model – they were motor homers – and they encouraged Sarah and Craig to give it a go. When Craig had retired from his work in reinsurance and Sarah had six months study leave from her job as a lecturer in languages, they decided to travel around Australia while Sarah wrote up the research she'd been doing. She wrote ten research papers during that time, an extraordinary number by any standard. As a result, she's decided she will never have a computer in her motor home again!

After Sarah returned to work, an unexpected offer of early retirement catapulted her into officially retiring at the age of 55. 'It took me about 20 seconds to adjust. I'd been working long hours and experiencing a high level of stress. I felt absolutely no sense of loss, but rather immense personal gain. I do have a recurring dream about forgetting to go to a lecture or a class (something I never did in fact) from which I wake in panic.'

They left immediately for another trip around Australia in their motor home and have never really stopped living the nomadic life. In 2001, with the help and advice of other couples following a similar path they purchased a second-hand motor home in Europe. The joys of the countryside, and the French and Spanish villages they visited, ensured they were soon addicted to this new way of life. 'Retirement was utterly different from what we expected', says Sarah. For Craig it was 'Better than I ever imagined; should have started earlier'. They continue to spend around half the year travelling.

Sarah still holds fast to her identity as a language teacher, even though her only connection with that of late has been speaking French and Spanish on their travels: 'I've been a language teacher since I was 18 – that's me! At night I still plan imaginary lessons and courses that I'll offer for free in retirement villages or elsewhere when we return home.'

What is it about motor homing that has such a strong appeal for them? Sarah hardly had to think about her answer:

It's everybody's dream come true and it really suits us. Our friends visit us – nine lots visited us on our first European trip – and that's great fun. Being in the motor home with Craig is like our being in a physical cocoon. We love being away from everything with time to keep fit, and to do ordinary things like the crossword, and also have time to explore new places and other ways of life. The framework for our travel is visiting wine areas, churches and sporting events. We can watch the world soccer cup or the Tour de France in real time in pubs or bars.

Similar things are emphasised by Craig:

It's like being on a boat. Everything has its place and has to be put back there. I am careful not to tread on Sarah's space as she is with mine. I love the sense of freedom, the driving, and the general experience of different cultures and their wine and food – we are far from passive travellers. And I have time to read in a way I could never do at home.

When I ask about the disadvantages, Sarah says the frustration of not being able to get on with normal life is the main thing she notices. She thinks of herself as an emergency person when they are at home – doing stints with meals on wheels,

Lifeline, and other voluntary work, and lots of babysitting. 'We fit twelve months of activity into six.'

She also mentions that leaving the family behind ('Your 'self' alters a bit when there are grandchildren') makes it more difficult. Using skype to keep in touch makes a big difference, but she admits their children are not really happy about it. 'My daughter hates it. She bemoans the fact that we are missing out on the grandchildren.' Sarah says they keep making plans about what they will do 'when we settle down', but they haven't settled down yet and she wonders now if they ever will.

~

Angela and Brad M decided to retire at roughly the same time. Angela had been working part time in aged care, after a career as a diversional therapist, and her husband, Brad, had worked for Sydney Water for 41 years. When they were first married, they went camping every holiday. Then they progressed to a campervan, so buying a caravan (a 15-metre pop top caravan that they tow with a Ford Fairmont) was a natural extension of this. As Angela explains, they'd always planned to spend their time travelling in retirement:

> We are grey nomads. We own a small caravan and go away for three months each year plus smaller trips away as well. My favourite part of caravanning is sitting outside and listening to the birds singing while reading a book or patch-working. I take along my sewing machine and laptop for downloading photos, using the quilting program, the

genealogy program and trip notes, and watching DVDs. Brad plays golf at all the different courses.

They plan where they want to go, but decide as they tour where to stay and for how long. The first year they retired they went to Europe for three months and used the van for 24 weeks. On their last three-month trip they covered 6400 kilometres around Australia. National parks, gorges, botanical gardens and historical towns are favourite destinations.

What is it that draws them to this way of life? Angela describes how she feels:

> So many people retire with no plan and get sick of the daily routine and each other. We have the same interests and love seeing new places and meeting people – so we don't get sick of each other. Most people you meet along the way are so interesting and friendly. As you drive along the roads, caravaners wave to each other – it doesn't happen with the motor homers, which is strange. I find now that Sydney is too fast and has so much traffic – I need to get out of it at least once every three months.

They hope to caravan for another 20 years, but realise it will depend on their health. When they are not touring, Angela's life is full of activities, many of them community oriented, and she finds there are never enough hours in the day. Her experience working in aged care has made her realise how important quality of life can be:

You need contact with other people or you lose your social and communication skills. You need to be physically and mentally active in retirement, and have things that make you get out of bed and out the door. No one knows what's around the corner so you need to enjoy life while you can.

Choosing a nomadic life of the kind suggested here may not be for the faint hearted, but once people begin the journey it appears to be an addictive lifestyle. The repercussions the choice has for everyday life no doubt shows up more clearly in the periods spent not travelling, and people find varying ways to deal with the problems that arise. The expense of this choice is another issue that may be of concern, but as it is a way of life that can be followed in style or more humbly, as well as extensively or more occasionally, then this is probably a matter of individual decision and negotiation.

Staying put

There are also those who choose to stay put for as long as possible. In fact, the urge to stay put can be so powerful that you hear some people saying they hope that when the time comes they'll be carried out feet first from their present home. I once met a couple who'd built their house with extra wide door frames specifically for an easy exit for this very purpose!

Tony and I don't plan on going to these lengths, but we are an example of people who'd like to stay put. This doesn't mean we haven't thought about the pleasures of villa versus city, seaside versus countryside, or moving to another less expensive, less trafficky state. In fact, we usually explore the idea of moving to whatever spot we visit on holiday. But when we get home again we decide we don't really want to move. And to our surprise, moving to an apartment looks as if it would be just as costly as continuing to live where we are now, and would provide us with much less space, something that, contrary to popular opinion, we seem to need more of, rather than less, as we grow older.

We would like to live near our children and grandchildren, but as two of them live in a different country, and one is in a different state, and they may not stay where they are for long, it is too radical a move to make. We've spent a long time getting our house right for our style of life. Now that I am retired I revel in doing some gardening from time to time; I love having the space to paint and do my decoupage and other hobbies (should I say 'plan to do'... I often don't get around to these pursuits); and finally we do have room to house the family when they come to visit, a mixed blessing some might say, but one we don't want to be without. Of course, our plans may change by necessity, or even whim, but for now we love being where we are.

Whether or not to move house after retirement concerns everyone in some shape or form. Many people find the removal of the restrictions imposed by a working life frees up possibilities of different lifestyles. Some take the chance to follow their dreams and do something unusual, while others follow a more conservative path. The latter can take consolation from the words of the Roman poet Horace: 'They change their view of the sky, not their soul, who run across the sea' (*'Caelum non animum mutant qui trans mare currunt'*).

Many of the moves people make work out well, but some go wrong, even badly wrong. On the other hand, being able to move house is not an option that is available to everyone. Circumstances (elderly parents, ill health, lack of finances) can dictate what options are available, and not having the freedom to make that choice can prove limiting and frustrating.

To move or not to move is clearly an important decision that touches on many of our most powerful instincts, desires and needs. Yet however much you think through the possibilities when making your decision, there will be aspects that remain out of your control or that turn out differently from the way you anticipated. Making the right choice involves a certain amount of luck in relation to factors such as whether you are able to sell your home when you need to, what is available for purchase at the time and so on. A substantial degree of compromise also seems to be necessary in relation to decisions of this kind – whether it is choosing to give up something in order to keep something else, making deals about priorities with a partner, or guessing at how your life might change over the stretch of time ahead and catering for the possibilities.

In Chapter 3 we looked at how people initially responded to retirement and heard about what they felt, thought and did in the early years. In the next chapter we hear from those who have been retired for longer periods of time, ranging from five years, when the newness of the state is wearing off, to 30 years or more when retirement has become familiar as a way of life.

Down
the track

The attempt to hold on to, or judge oneself by,
youthful parameters blinds us to the new strengths
and possibilities emerging in ourselves.

The Fountain of Age, Betty Frieden, 1994

If Jacques, the melancholic cynic in Shakespeare's *As you Like It*, were philosophising today instead of in 1599, when life spans were shorter and old age was arrived at much earlier, he'd need to revise his comically gloomy account of the later stages of a man's life:

> *The sixth age shifts*
> *Into the lean and slipper'd pantaloon,*
> *With spectacles on nose and pouch on side;*
> *His youthful hose, well sav'd, a world too wide*
> *For his shrunk shank; and his big manly voice,*
> *Turning again toward childish treble, pipes*

And whistles in his sound. Last scene of all,
That ends this strange eventful history
Is second childishness and mere oblivion;
Sans teeth, sans eyes, sans taste, sans everything.

(Act II, Scene VII, lines 157–166)

The equivalent sixth age in the twenty-first century is when people are in the heart of their retirement. They may be well aware that 'shrunk shanks' loom and that the 'sans teeth' stage is not as far away as it used to be. But, for the most part, these people are actively engaged in playing their parts on this world's stage. What they are thinking, feeling and doing presents a very different picture from that conjured up by Jacques' speech.

Euphoria, where are you?

As we saw in Chapter 3, the first few years of retirement often bring quite powerful euphoric or pleasurable feelings at being released from the pressures of work. What happens when more years have passed? Do these feelings remain intense, become a pleasure revisited from time to time, or do they evaporate? And what happens to those who initially feel disappointment, even despair about their retired state. Do things improve for them? What do people do with their time when they are in it for the longer haul?

Words such as 'joy', 'delight' and 'elation' continue to

be chosen to describe how people feel as they get further down the track of retirement. Even after 21 years of being retired Ceridwen C is in no doubt about the whereabouts of her earlier euphoric feelings – they are ever-present as they are for many others. She unconsciously echoes Crystal C's earlier words when she says, 'I still wake up with a smile every day because I don't have to get up and go to work.' Mick N, who took early retirement in 1998 from his role as manager of a US firm supplying wood preservatives in Australia, puts it a little differently: 'For about six months I was concerned I mightn't be able to afford early retire-ment, but this anxiety had nothing to do with the state of retirement itself. My dominant feeling was elation at my release from drudgery and that has never gone away.'

Even Marcus H, the former professional rugby league player, who describes himself as a 'pommy pragmatist', throws in a few superlatives when describing how he feels seven years after his retirement. He migrated from England to Australia in 1962, became a sales manager in the build-ing industry after time spent in the army and the navy, and took an offer of early retirement at 61 in 2000. He had few regrets about leaving work – he disliked the corporate fad of total quality management of the 1990s; he was feeling 'a bit redundant anyway'; and as his sense of identity was more closely connected with his sporting career than his working life, there was no great sense of loss to complicate matters. Running out of money was an anxiety, but other than that he was 'elated' when the time came to give up work. Marcus identifies the situation of not being directed to do things as the major source of his satisfaction. 'Having the freedom to choose what to do and when you can do it is the bonus. I love being outdoors and now I can be as often as I like. I don't feel as if I'm pressured into anything. I enjoy being retired hugely.'

I asked Sonia S, a librarian who left work in 2000 ('I could own a dog at last!'), if retirement gets better as it goes along. She replied, 'It's hard to say because it was great from the start. It changes with new interests and discoveries opening up ... having the freedom to live such a crowded life is wonderful.' Many feel a steady sense of contentment with their lot. Christine O, who retired in 1998, cites reasons for her pleasure in being retired that many confirm. 'I love being retired. Because I'm in control of my time, no pressure from others, and doing the things I want to do.'

What of those who struggle with initial feelings of displacement or even discontent? Franz T certainly misses his work as the manager of a large government body, particularly 'its pressure and activity, and more significantly the collegiality and stimulation of the place'. His life is now filled with pleasurable and useful pursuits, but feelings of a loss of purpose recur from time to time:

> There is no doubt that one has to get to grips with the huge change of role that takes place. One minute you feel as if you are central to important activities and the next you realise that you are not even peripheral any more to those activities. And all you can do is accept the situation and

perhaps have a little moan to anyone who might listen. I exaggerate but it is a little like losing your purpose for being.

When Dymphna N retired in 2000 she felt 'like a deflated cushion' for at least three months. She wryly acknowledges there are some good things about retirement: 'There is time to reinvent yourself – I got a new knee, for example. And you get time to pursue interests – read, play the piano, garden. I don't just sit around waiting for life to happen.' But she still suffers from fairly acute feelings of loss of purpose and of status. 'All days are alike. I still miss the daily interaction with others, the camaraderie and rapport, and even the frisson you experience with certain people. I like being alive, but sometimes I feel there is no reason to get up.'

In a follow-up conversation she expressed surprise that she'd been so negative during our interview. In fact, she does all sorts of interesting things and leads quite a full life, but on that day she was seeing retirement as 'the deserts of vast eternity' and feeling she needed 'to disturb the monotony of living in lotus land'. It is good in a way that I caught her in that mood as her thoughts give a voice to an underlying fear that some people repress: retirement can be boring and monotonous, and it can make you feel purposeless.

Regrets and reflections

What of the other more negative emotions and thoughts people experience in the early years of retirement? Do they disappear over time? Do new sources of discontent emerge? On the whole, I found that the longer you spend in retirement the more likely it is that the negative feelings you initially experience begin to fade or take on a different perspective. As the years go by, anger and irritation with the workplace isn't mentioned as often, and the sense of mourning at leaving it behind seems to largely disappear. People express some concern about being out of the loop and out of touch with former colleagues, but soon reconcile themselves to this and welcome the greater amounts of time they can spend with friends, family and the other new connections they now have time to establish.

Feelings of a loss of purpose do seem to colour the retirement picture a few shades darker for quite a few people; and guilt continues to rear its ugly head, though maybe with less intensity and from different causes than in the early years. Madeleine M, a former linguist, says, 'In one sense I haven't adjusted yet [she retired 15 years ago]. I still don't like it much. If you have always worked, as I have, then not working seems a bit of a waste of time.' Mick N confesses to 'guilt pangs about not doing some useful social service activity,' as does Franz T:

> It's all very well to do things one enjoys, such as read the papers, pursue cultural and hobby interests, but they all

tend to be self-centred and not completely satisfying.

There is a touch of the Protestant guilt about all of this, engendered, I think, by my father who worked on the farm until he lost his licence at 86. Mind you, I'm not really interested in community volunteering etc., apart from teaching a little bit here and there. I do enjoy my little primary kids and even their teachers. On the other hand, I'm not inclined to return to full-time, paid work because that would interfere with the self-centred and relaxing interests that appeal to my lazy side.

Marcus H takes a different view. Brought up in a pit mining area and conscious of the way the working environment declined in the Thatcher era, he thinks that after 40 odd years in the workforce you deserve the reward of retirement. The only guilt he would feel, he says, is if he wasn't busy doing things: 'and as I always am, I feel no guilt at all'.

'Boredom' and 'restlessness' are other states mentioned very occasionally. Those who experience these feelings find them hard to combat. They often want to start a project of some kind or go back to part-time work, but somehow they talk themselves out of beginning. There is also the ever-present fear of ill health. As Dymphna N states, 'Another thing that obsesses you is declining health. You can't defeat it but you can combat it. It's best to cultivate a carapace and not talk about it.' Not advice everyone follows. When Mick N has his quarterly lunch with former workmates, they 'enjoy catching up, comparing retirement experiences and diagnosing one another's ailments!'

Despair about the way workplaces are heading (corporate takeovers, faddish restructures and so on) is a frequent cause of concern in the early years, but people don't worry so much about this when it no longer affects them personally. The view that things are going from bad to worse in world affairs, and anything else you can think of, often said to characterise the attitude of the older generation, is not an attitude I encountered very often. I do recall one amusing conversation with Josh T, an author of fiction, who has been retired for well over 25 years, in which he said: 'Name me one thing that has improved over time. You can't. Nothing is better. Perhaps ice cream has improved, but that's about it!'

Pieter P who came to Australia from Holland in 1959 when he was 15, feels very strongly that learning to adjust to change is a vital part of ageing gracefully in retirement. When Pieter arrived he couldn't speak English. He began his working life as a messenger boy with a chain of jewellery stores, worked his way up to being in charge of the clock department, and eventually ran his own financial planning business until retiring in 1999. Pieter sees himself as a rather serious person and attributes this to his European background, where war and depression made such an impact on the lives of his parents' generation. Keeping things in perspective is very important to him. 'It's no use saying politics is getting worse or the world is going to be a terrible place for your grandchildren. You need to find the positives in the changes that are occurring and learn to adapt.'

On the whole it seems that as time goes on, the euphoria of giving up work and the strong feelings of enjoyment and satisfaction that follow are powerful forces that show little sign of diminishing. In addition, the negative emotions initially experienced tend to lose their sting. Different doubts and anxieties do sometimes arise, but there are many compensatory pleasures that people acknowledge as they move on into the heart of their retirement.

Doing things differently

How much do people's priorities change through retirement, and are there significant changes in the way people spend their time? Exercising and taking care of health matters continue to have a very high priority. Many carry on with their regular gym sessions, walking, swimming, Pilates and so on. Golf, tennis and bowls are mentioned quite often, and some venture into new sports such as canoeing where 'you have to practise 365-degree turns!' I was amused to come across a comment made by the wife of a retired cop in Peter Corris's novel *Master's Mates* (2003, Allen & Unwin, Sydney, p. 179): 'He misses it [his work as a cop] all sometimes. I can tell. I see him going off to golf and I know that it's a substitute for what was his real life.'

Planned and unplanned travel ('We talk and do nothing about travel and then suddenly go when the opportunity pops up') continues throughout retirement. Other creative pursuits such as gardening, cooking and painting that emerge as new interests for many during their retirement often prove to be lasting, and indeed some people become quite expert in these areas. Reading is a hot favourite and some report being members of book groups for over two decades or more; most mention reading newspapers and journals to keep up with politics and world affairs. Whether or not sex becomes more or less important is not something I asked people about, fearing it would be an invasion of privacy, not to mention a minefield that would be tricky to negotiate. I can report, however, that one person I interviewed confided that for her 'The nicest sex I've ever had was after I turned 70'.

Theatre and gallery, and to a lesser extent concert visits, are still regularly mentioned. An interest in plotting family trees and recording and writing family histories also takes root with many retired people, though not everyone succumbs to curiosity about the past. Marcus H says: 'I'm interested in it and I mean to do it, but I can't get myself going. I don't want to spend time on all that detail. I think I'll end up spending weeks or months on doing this thing, and I resist.'

Volunteer work has a very high profile with those who are 'down the track'. Choosing something of particular interest to you that uses your special talents is likely to work better than doing good just for the sake of it, according to most volunteers. Sometimes volunteering may be as simple as regularly helping a friend ('every fortnight I meet a friend and workmate who does not drive, and I take her to the hairdresser and shopping'), or it may involve more extensive work with those in need – helping out with ambulance services; being a mentor or peer adviser for the blind; assisting in recovery from mental health problems; taking groups of people with dementia for outings; helping with aged care; and being on boards of organisations. As Annike R who is involved in several of these activities, explains: 'I feel a great sense of achievement from the work I'm doing. I make others happy and so I can be happy myself through that.'

Most people acknowledge that having a structure to their days, weeks and years evolves over time, whether or not they plan it that way. Many can say what they will be doing each day of the week and in the months, if not the years, ahead. A time and motion study Pieter P carried out in his business gave him insights into time management, and how easy it is to waste it. He now employs this knowledge to help organise his use of time in retirement. His days are full and varied, he builds in time to help out family members, and he makes time for developing closer friendships now in a way he felt unable to when working. 'Looking after shares and investments involves everyday work', he adds. 'In my mind I feel as if I am still useful. I feel as if I'm managing my own business.'

Christine O says she is more relaxed about doing things, though she does have more structure in her weekly life than when she initially retired, deciding to settle on around one or two activities each day:

As I have become older and the body/mind are not in tip top shape, I do not feel I have to achieve so much with my time. I have hung up my ski boots, deciding this year was to be the last of my heli skiing holidays in Canada. It is close to being an extreme sport and I haven't the strength to compete with the young guns. Now it's bridge and just golf. Having some spare time I got involved in golf club politics and got elected to the Board (the only woman in its 100-year history). I feel my years in the public service have served me well for committee work. And my expectations are more realistic with experience and age.

A pattern others follow is not to plan, to go with the flow. This is a style that comes naturally to Mick N. 'I don't think there is any serious structure to my use of time. I tend to be project driven and what I do and when I do it is determined by projects in hand and how far behind I am with them, or by how overstuffed the email inbox has become. There is no allocation of time to particular activities.' Sometimes a pattern that you may adopt or fall into will turn out not to really suit your nature. It can take effort and imagination to make changes, but as Barbara N, who retired from her demanding job in the business world in New York in 1999 confirms, it can be worth taking the trouble:

I thought that when I retired, I'd be happy just relaxing, but I still feel as though I have to be doing something 'useful' most of the day. I've finally given in to that. When I'm more active, I'm happier. I do enjoy my 'free' time, but I have to temper it with other things. I write and do volunteer work. I've had a few things published since I retired, and I'm currently taking my second writing workshop. I also volunteer for the local oral history project.

On the other hand, the best laid plans often go awry as many of the things people imagine they will do in terms of organising their possessions and their lives continue to be put off for a rainy day.

Friends, family and other networks

The pastime that increases for nearly all retired people is that of spending time with friends and/or family. I add the 'or' because a very small percentage say they like to avoid family where possible and to concentrate on friends. Networks of workmates often fall away ('I was happy to close the book and look forward to new things'), though sometimes not quickly enough according to Franz T. 'I very deliberately cut myself off from the workplace because I'd seen too many people return to various roles and make pests of themselves because they assumed, wrongly I think, that they were still needed.' Contacts developed through retirement interests often fill the gap left by connections with former colleagues.

Spending time with old friends and cultivating new friendships is high on most people's lists, though the sexes tend to go about this in different ways. My husband says men enjoy 'low maintenance friendships that you can pick up where you left off, whenever that time occurs – yesterday or 50 years back – no difference!' He is exaggerating, of course, but what is clear is that women favour the high-maintenance variety of friendships and use phone, email, and lunch and coffee engagements to this end. Only one man I interviewed said he enjoyed lengthy phone calls with friends, and only half a dozen of the males I spoke to said they regularly meet with friends for coffee or a meal; meeting up at the pub sometimes serves this function.

Mitchell N is something of an exception. He is often the only male attending activities such as Pilates and bridge with his wife Katy. 'He is an honorary girl at bridge', says Katy grinning. Mitchell adds: 'I like these women. Most have lost their husbands, but that's no reason for me not to be there.' Another unusual aspect to the friendship pattern of this married couple is that the husbands of a group of Katy's friends have formed their own men's group. According to Mitchell:

> Katy got a group together when Ita Buttrose asked her to gather some interesting women for a project she was running. It turned out on the six degrees of separation rule that some of the husbands knew each other already. When the women met we decided to meet too – we go out to a restaurant together. Now in retirement we still do that and we meet up as couples fairly regularly as well.

Male and female attitudes to joining communal groups

and organised activities are also rather different. Male re-
luctance to take part in formal learning situations is well
documented. The growing success of community sheds in
Australia, places where men, about 75 per cent of whom
are retired, gather for hands-on activities and talking with
mates offers a different kind of learning space. Associate
Professor Barry Golding of the University of Ballarat, lead
author of the 2007 national survey into the role these sheds
play, states:

> Sheds allow men to tap into the essence of being 'blokes'...
> One of the themes in the responses to our questions was
> that men enjoy the opportunity to 'get out of the house' –
> and almost all 'feel at home' in the shed. They also like the
> practical learning they can gain at sheds – and the fact that
> there is no compulsion.

Probus and community clubs, voluntary work, educational
organisations, hobby classes, book groups, sewing circles
and other organised social activities provide multiple
opportunities for developing new friendships. The fact
that more women than men choose to participate in these
activities tends to make men highly prized collectibles in
this context.

Neighbours are another source of friendships, particularly when people spend a lot of time at home. Matthew B,
who lives in London, says: 'Having lived in the same house
for 25 years, we have good close contacts with adjoining
families. We help each other out when needed and gen-

erally get on well. Our neighbours, incidentally, include Greek, Italian and West Indian people as well as Londoners.' For those who enjoy more solitary pursuits, maintaining and developing new friendships can have its difficulties. As Dymphna N, who is currently preparing for her Licentiate Trinity College London Certificate in Piano, explains:

> Playing the piano is a very solitary occupation, but it is an identity thing and I could never stop it. When you leave a workplace, relationships change and it is usually no good going back. Several of my old friends have moved away overseas and elsewhere. When I visit them they too seem to have changed. I don't know what it is, but I think I must have an emetic effect on people!

Soon after Mick N retired he taught himself how to develop a website and a system of communicating via a monthly newsletter and email conferencing with people who share his philosophical and spiritual interests. Communicating electronically puts Mick in touch with an evolving line of friends and acquaintances who share his interests in what he loosely describes as 'recovering that aspect of our being which our social conditioning denies'. And, as he says on the site: 'the answer to the question of what I really, really am is what these [web] pages are about'. This work consumes a great deal of his time and energy. 'In terms of time allocated it is a full-time "job". I'm only saved from being completely taken over by the computer by my other addictions, such as DIY projects like rain harvesting, and my interest in wood turning and carving.'

Mick's use of technologies illustrates their potential for putting quite a different face on the retirement experience for many people. Those who retire now can do hundreds of things electronically that were not possible, or even imagined, until quite recently. Developments in technologies enable people to lead lives of greater convenience through, for example, banking online, or having detailed, current information about anything from tortellini to travel available on tap at home. Technologies now offer the means to contact people wherever they are located in a variety of ways and in a minimum of time. Almost every day you hear of some new avenue that developing technologies is opening up to consumers. I've just been reading about 'virtual volunteering', for example, something I hadn't realised was a widespread enterprise involving numerous people using their skills from home to help others in a variety of ways. As technologies continue to evolve, further opportunities are accruing to change the way we live.

New responsibilities

Changing social and work patterns make it quite possible, particularly for those nearer the baby boom end of the retirement scale, to be in demand as carers of family members. Caring for elderly parents or a partner can be time-consuming and difficult, particularly when ill health is involved; caring for young grandchildren can be physically demanding and a considerable challenge. If you are thinking this generation gets a double whammy, caught between sets of potentially heavy responsibilities, you are not wrong, and it looks set to stay this way for quite some time.

The changes to traditional family patterns that began last century mean there are many new trends in partnering and child rearing. People find themselves involved in grandparenting and step grandparenting roles of kinds that would not have been likely in the past. These roles vary across cultures, but the trend towards multicultural societies makes the mingling of families of different race more common nowadays.

Blood connections with grandchildren are exceptionally powerful, but so too are other kinds of bonds. This was confirmed by conversations with several interviewees. One couple was rejoicing in grandchildren being brought up by their daughter and her same-sex partner who'd each given birth to a child from an anonymous common donor. Another couple talked of the ease and pleasure with which they'd adopted the role of grandparents for children of their daughter's new partner from a previous marriage.

On the whole, women take on more of the day-by-day duties, but many of the men I interviewed are, or have been in the past, significantly involved in caring for grandchildren. Raymond K, for example, says he's become closer to his three sons and six grandsons since his wife, Maggie, died. He carries out grandparent duties in ways he'd never anticipated. 'I was not an enormously devoted father and didn't contribute much. Now I do. I didn't feel as needed before as I do now.'

Both singles and partnered grandparents speak about their grandchildren as a major priority in their lives, though there are some who avoid the babysitting role for various reasons. 'I was shocked to be asked to baby sit, and my daughter was hurt and shocked when I said I wouldn't. I did double time with my two. I didn't want to get into the trap of being a childminder in the early stages anyway'; 'I'm not the type for regular babysitting and I worry my ex-wife might be a bit peeved perhaps if I intervened'. In 2007, when the coalition government in Australia announced its plan of allowing working grandparents to take up to a year of unpaid leave to help care for their grandchildren, not all grandparents responded positively.

Grandparenting is, however, almost unanimously described as one of the greatest joys that life has to offer. People struggle to put into words what exactly makes it such a fulfilling role. They fall back on the old familiar 'it's because you can hand them back' explanation, and there's some truth in this, but it doesn't begin to touch on the special qualities that make the relationship such a winner. Paul Keating, a former Australian prime minister, recently said becoming a grandparent 'changed my whole life', a not unusual response. And Thomas Kenneally, the Australian novelist, puts it another way: 'As for my grandchildren I planned what Evelyn Waugh planned. That I would see them for five minutes every Easter or Christmas. And if they behaved well I'd give them a boiled sweet. But, I didn't know that I'd fall in love with them, you know?' (ABC *Talking Heads*, 30 July 2007)

Some describe the feeling of continuity that grand-children evoke ('these are mine; I'm in them'; 'she's here because of me') as creating a sense of fulfilment, even achievement. Being in touch with young minds with their innocence and curiosity and natural acceptance of life as play is another pleasurable part of grandparenting. Vera P enjoys the way 'their sayings become part of your life'; Katrina G thinks they are 'like climbing plants that wrap their little tendrils around you'; and as Mick N puts it: 'Grandchildren come along and child's play turns up again'. The pleasure of their acceptance is a delight that Edna M recognises: 'They want to see you. They love you uncondi-tionally; it doesn't happen often in life.'

Research supports the view that many grandparents are involved in caring for their grandchildren. A 2004 survey by the Council on the Ageing in Australia claims more than 30 000 children under 14 were living with their grand-parents. These situations, often brought about by trauma or tragedy, can be extraordinarily demanding and involve financial and emotional struggle. Part-time care of grand-children is also provided by many grandparents. In 2005, Australian Bureau of Statistics research figures indicate they were providing 39 per cent of the care arrangements for school-aged children.

Some grandparents from Western cultures talk about the guilt that accompanies the refusal of a request for child-minding; some take on more care of their grandchildren than they really want to accept, and may feel trapped and resentful; and the grandparents who do most of the child-minding often develop closer relationships with the family than do less willing or able grandparents. This can lead to jealousies and unhappy divisions. Others, such as Brenda S, manage to draw a line: 'I think if I gave up my research I might be swallowed up by grandchildren duties. It's wonder-ful to have five grandchildren, but one day a week is plenty.'

Advances in technologies make communications with retired parents much easier from wherever their children and grandchildren are located. Whether this is a good thing or not is debateable. Most welcome, even depend heavily on, the newer technologies that make regular contact pos-sible when offspring live at a distance. Others, usually the grandfathers, complain these technologies allow children to 'dump' all their problems on their parents from wherever they are living. 'We used to protect our parents. Now we get the whole bloody thing.'

Another factor involved is the greater likelihood now of children growing into maturity, while their grandparents are still relatively young. With luck, this can allow for more extended, closer relationships to develop. Many of my con-temporaries remember their grandparents with affection, but they tended to die quite early on in their lives. There were no grandparents at all in my life. I recall being taken to see my mother's father on his deathbed when I was about six, but that is my only memory. In a weird twist of fate, I discovered through the Internet that my mother's mother was born in 1886, but had not died until 1981 when I was 37. She was never mentioned at home and I had no idea she was alive, apparently a not altogether uncommon practice with relatives in past times, as I have since discovered. My own grandchildren, the eldest of whom is nearing his teens, have all their grandparents and step grandparents alive, all vitally interested in their wellbeing, and all hoping to be around for a long time yet, a much more common pattern today.

In some Asian societies there are different expectations of the grandparent role. I recently had first-hand experience of this when we visited my husband's son, James, and his Vietnamese wife, Snow, and our newly born grandson, Max, at their home in Kuala Lumpur. Snow's parents (neither of whom speak English) and another daughter, Thuy, flew in from Vietnam as soon as Max was born. They clearly saw it as their pleasurable duty to devote themselves for several months to the care of Max, and Snow's sister, Thuy, was even willing to stay on for a year to act as childminder while Snow went back to work. I asked Thuy how she felt about this. 'I'm young, I'm only 23, I'll have time for my career and other things later. In our society we help each other when babies are born.'

I also talked with Snow about the different expectations Vietnamese society has in relation to retirement and the role of grandparents. She explained that in Vietnam parents assume their children will provide support and care for them in their old age as very few people have superannuation funds. In return, grandparents expect to look after grandchildren and help with care of the home. From my observations, Snow's family was utterly devoted to their role as child carers and saw it as offering a new and rewarding purpose for living. Our conversation brought home to me very directly the extent to which individual choices in relation to family responsibilities are shaped by the values and beliefs of the societies of which we are a part.

Spending time with family, friends and others who share your interests is clearly an essential part of retirement for many people. But most people also feel the need to have some way to express their individuality. This can take many forms and may involve building on neglected skills, fine tuning existing talents, or finding a new direction of some kind. For some this expands into a time-consuming hobby or project, or even a new career. In the next section we look at three people who have had this kind of experience.

New careers, new projects

People who change direction by beginning a new 'career' or becoming involved in various projects after they retire are often envied by others, not for the projects in themselves, but because of the sense of purpose and fulfilment they bring. To be successful, these endeavours usually draw on an individual's talents and abilities that transplant well into a new environment. Some examples of projects I came across that have been successfully sustained over time during 'retirement' include starting a coffee plantation from scratch, learning how to use new technologies to record the behaviour of deer, and building a new branch of the University of the Third Age.

Meredith J retired from her job as a cataloguer at the Film and Television School in New South Wales in 1993 at the age of 68. She is one of the 'I still wake up and feel pleased I don't have to go to work' brigade. She even thinks retirement improves over time. 'If you can discount illness [Meredith has been diagnosed with multiple myeloma and her husband has spinal problems that are making walking difficult for him], then I think I can say retirement has got better as it has gone on and I have certainly had a most rewarding time.'

She and her husband, Will, a former government architect, bought 28 acres of land in Lismore, New South Wales, in 1974 with the plan of moving there in retirement and using the rent from their Sydney flat as income. Taxes were high on the land and in order to get rural rates they set up a five-year plan to build a coffee plantation. When I asked Meredith whether she viewed herself as a retired person or as taking her working life in a new direction she had no hesitation in her response: 'I was definitely retired. Even though I recall the exhaustion of planting 1300 coffee plants and soaking in a hot bath afterwards watching the red earth soak out of me, I felt retired. It was my choice. Time was my own and I was no longer on a treadmill.'

As soon as they moved to Lismore, Meredith joined the Northern Rivers branch of the University of the Third Age, with over 600 members, where she followed interests in science, maths, philosophy, Latin and history, and enjoyed the social clubs – a dance group, a wine tasting group, tennis, music and so on. She started a book group, which is still going, and made many new friends.

After eight busy years, Meredith and Will had to sell the coffee farm and move back to their Sydney flat. Meredith still lives a very active life in spite of financial difficulties and health problems. She joined the Sydney U3A; she reads ('especially *New Scientist*'); she does part-time research for an author (Daisy Bates' third husband was a recent subject); she takes part in the *Australian Longitudinal Study on Women's Health*, a landmark 20-year study that provides information on women across three generations; and she is 'always on hand to pick up the grandchildren'. I've mentioned before the extraordinarily courageous spirit of many retired people with serious illnesses – Meredith exemplifies that spirit.

~

We have a very interesting plumber. He is knowledgeable about an extraordinary number of things ranging from Islamic art to archery (he was an Australian junior champion in this sport) to deer farming. While plumbing is his bread and butter, his heart is in the outdoors and the natural world, and he says that one day he hopes to farm deer full time. Bob M introduced me to his mother, Joan, when he learned I was writing this book.

Joan was about to have some renovations completed at her home near the northern beaches on the day of our interview, but she still made me welcome and we soon settled down in two large armchairs in front of the fire to talk about Joan's life in retirement. We detoured for a time to her early life as she recollected it so vividly – I was captivated by the trace of an Irish lilt and her gift for storytelling.

Joan was third youngest of a family of ten children born in Northern Ireland. She left school when she was 12 and took her first job 'packaging handkerchiefs'. She soon noticed the girls who were machinists earned more than she did, so she learned how to earn her livelihood in that way.

At the time, it was the custom in Ireland for children to hand over their pay packets to their mother ('until we got engaged'), and Joan remembers getting two shillings back from her wage of £1.10.0 and saving up to buy the first coat she'd ever chosen for herself, 'a red coat with a belt'. Later she bought herself a bicycle.

Joan married Robert M, a mechanic for an eye care company, and on 1 December 1972, the day Gough Whitlam was elected prime minister of Australia, they arrived in Sydney with their three children. Two of Robert's sisters – he has ten surviving siblings from his mother's 25 pregnancies – had come earlier and he was keen to join them. Joan remained reluctant to leave her home until the day a petrol station exploded before her eyes. The 'troubles' sprang to life right in front of her in a personal way and she changed her mind about staying there.

After coming to Sydney the family had to work hard to make their way. Joan says being retired is a much easier life and she enjoys the contrast, though she says Robert, who retired some years after she did in 2002, feels very differently: 'He is lost. He does a bit of maintenance work for real estate agents now, but he hates retirement and says it is the worst thing that can happen to anybody.'

When Joan retired she thought she'd spend her time sewing. 'Well, that's gone out the window hasn't it! I do some sewing occasionally – make pyjamas or dress-ups for the grandchildren. But it's unusual for me to spend much time at it. I'm really surprised.'

She does, however, like to have some projects on the go ('If days go by and I don't do something, I think of it as lost time'), as well as doing regular things such as aqua classes, community club activities, 'scrap-booking', crosswords and seeing her eight grand-children ('I minded the youngest for one day a week just because I wanted to'). Most of the projects she works on are connected with helping out family members and involve learning new skills – using a digital camera, learning to video and edit, and using skype (she chats to her brothers in Ireland, England and Scotland by this means); and next on the list is learning to build a website. She is partly self-taught ('I learn from asking'), but she also attends local colleges and other classes to learn the skills she needs.

Her 'deer' project involves photographing and filming the deer at her son's property, 'Dongadale Deer Park' ('Dongadale' is a Swahili word meaning 'valley between two rocky ridges; Donga – as in 'Wodonga' – is a slang word for 'bush' that Australian soldiers brought back from the Boer War). She describes her progress:

> At first I'd pick a tree and sit there, but you can sit for hours and not see the deer. I found that in my ordinary clothes I couldn't get near enough for a good photo. But they are colour blind as far as orange goes, so that was the secret. Now I dress my tripod and myself in orange – I have orange wet weather gear as well – and I get much closer to them.
>
> The wilder deer are very elusive. You need a zoom so I went for a DVD video camera with a 30-metre zoom, learned how to use and edit the film, and now have lots of footage.

Two of Joan's photos have been used to challenge the literature on deer in ways that have implications for how they are handled and managed. And Bob has a dream of using his mother's accumulated work to create a David Attenborough-style documentary narrated by a relative of theirs with a beautiful Anglo Indian voice.

What is it about the project that appeals to her? 'Well, it's quite unexpected. I never imagined such a thing. I like going to the farm with my husband, or being there with Bob while he's working. I enjoy sitting in the middle of three and a half thousand acres. I enjoy the filming, but mostly I want to do it for Bob, to keep a record for him.'

~

In his work *On Old Age*, the Roman statesman, Cicero, remarks: 'I do not know any part of life that is passed more agreeably than the learned leisure of a virtuous old age'. In the twenty-first century many people still turn to learning, often in ways undreamed of in 50 BCE, as a valuable and productive way to spend their time.

Matthew B, who retired from his position on the management team of an Anglo French library supply company in 1995 after a highly successful career in the library world, lives in London with his wife, Genevieve, who is still 'a busy professional'. He is a forward-looking person whose view is that 'work was good but retirement is no punishment'.

When Matthew first retired he chose to take on more domestic chores, something he still happily does ('I've improved my cooking skills'; 'Mad as I am, I even gain satisfaction from tidying, cleaning, washing etc.'). He also decided to begin a branch of the University of the Third Age when he realised there was no such group in his area. He called a founding meeting to which 30 or so people turned up, and this was instrumental in their establishing a Waltham Forest U3A group. It now has 250 members and some 30 study groups on offer. At first, Matthew was involved as chairman and in committee work, something he has mostly given up now. He also began a music appreciation group, and a decade later runs two music groups who meet three times a month at his home.

His original connection with music began when his father took him to a wartime afternoon concert given by the Liverpool Philharmonic:

> After that I was hooked. I joined the music society at my Grammar school [the equivalent of a public school in Australia] run by my dear Mr Benson, our English teacher, who used to play the old 78s on a primitive radiogram. I was also fortunate in that the Halle Orchestra (Barbirolli conducting) and the Liverpool Philharmonic (Malcolm Sargeant) regularly came to Preston Guildhall so that I could listen to good music well performed.

Matthew's sons, one of whom was a brilliant child violinist, are all caught up with music through performing, composing, song writing and so on. Matthew says of himself as a performer: 'I'm totally talentless'. But he has a passion for music that never seems to dim and he loves to transmit his enthusiasm and knowledge of the world of music to his U3A groups. He describes his 20-volume *Grove's Dictionary of Music* as his 'major standby', and says it is a case of 'as I teach so I learn'.

You think you can't but you can

As you get older, the definition of what it is to be 'old' moves further ahead. When I was in my twenties I thought of my friend Neil, who was about three years older than me, as 'an older man'. Similarly, at age 24, I was 'an older woman' in the eyes of my friend Rhonda, who was 21 at the time. Now that I'm in my sixties I feel quite shocked and upset to see stories in the newspaper or on television that label people in their seventies as 'elderly'. I've been mentally reserving eighty and beyond for this label, but now with 'old' being the new 'young', even that age group seems quite youthful to me. It is of course partly that perceptions change as you grow older yourself, but it is also because people in this age bracket are ageing well, and doing more with their lives.

Unusual achievements of people in their eighties and nineties, and perhaps even in their hundreds (there are 25 000 centenarians in Japan, the fastest ageing society in the world, and 52 000 in the United States, for example), show us that it is possible to do some of the things we thought we probably couldn't in our later years. There are those in this age group who rock climb, skydive and paraglide; those who paint, write and perform; who graduate with Masters or PhD degrees on subjects that are quite new to them; and who carry out philanthropic and volunteer work right up until they reach their century.

A person whose accomplishments really bowled me over is Rex B who at 98 was still delivering meals on wheels, three times a week. He had to give up this voluntary work in 2007, as the council could not get insurance for him as a driver. I met Rex, originally a letter press printer, at a community club meeting and noticed it was he who at the end of the meeting did the packing away of all the technological equipment. He talked to me of helping his son on the farm and other feats I'd not imagined anyone undertaking when close to a 100 years of age. The community club regards him as their living treasure, as well they might.

It seems that when you are further down the track of retirement it continues to have many highlights and can bring with it a kind of contentment or fulfilment not previously experienced in life. There are, of course, those who suffer unfortunate and debilitating health problems and other setbacks that make for a difficult time; and sometimes a lack of purpose or the thought of 'shrunk shanks' clouds and overshadows the anticipation of future pleasures. But for most people it is a rewarding time, a time when new selves, and 'new strengths and possibilities' have a chance to emerge.

Three stories
and a postscript

Life isn't about finding yourself.
Life is about creating yourself.

Bernard Shaw

The idea that people who retire are just looking for the good life – freedom from responsibilities and holidays in the sun – is widely promoted through advertising and often echoed in what people say when they talk about their retirement fantasies. But this way of thinking offers a very limited perspective upon what people want to do with their lives during the years of their retirement. Not many want life to be a beach all the time. Many equally important, even overriding, desires are likely to surface. As the author of the epigraph of this chapter maintained: 'A perpetual holiday is a good working definition of hell'.

People talked to me about all sorts of needs, goals and desires other than those related to leisure and recreation. They included wanting to feel useful and needed, and to contribute in worthwhile ways to the welfare of family, friends and communities; to be able to use talents and abilities in new ways instead of letting them go to waste; and wanting to turn dreams suppressed or unattainable during ordinary working lives into something more tangible.

In this chapter we look in close up at three very different people and at how they have approached retirement: John Edwards, an Australian who had a career as a medical technologist and then as a professional hire car owner/driver, and who went on to walk the Kokoda Trail after a five-graft cardiac bypass operation; Jean Guillermo, a Frenchman and business executive in a multinational corporation, who developed a successful Blues Festival on the Seine; and Jane Sutherland, a former American academic and scholar who became a full-time exhibiting artist. By giving themselves to their new pursuits, these three found new meaning in their lives and recreated themselves in the process. Their stories record the doubts, hesitations, anxieties, changes of direction, rewards and moments of joy experienced along the way as they embarked on dramatically new journeys in their retirement years.

John Edwards: Kokoda Trail adventurer

The Kokoda Trail, a remote jungle track in Papua New Guinea, was the scene of a prolonged battle of endurance where Australian and New Guinean soldiers fought against the Japanese in World War 2. *Kokoda with Heart*, screened on Australian television in 2006, tells the story of three multiple cardiac bypass patients who tested their abilities and endurance by walking the Kokoda Trail. John Edwards, one of the three described by the media as 'ordinary Australians who wanted a second chance at life', had a five-graft bypass in 2002. I knew him as a professional hire car driver who occasionally drove us to the airport. We knew he was someone special even then, but this moving documentary left us in no doubt about his extraordinary qualities.

John agreed to my interviewing him at his home in the northern suburbs of Sydney where he and his wife, Jan, live with two dogs and four chooks, on five acres of land. I arrived in winter sunshine and settled by a log fire, drinking tea and eating homemade cakes. I left with eggs, limes and mandarins – that was the sort of interview it was. Here is John's story told in his own words.

FIRST RETIREMENT

Jan and I both worked as medical technologists at the CSIRO in Sydney for 26 years. Towards the end of that time the culture was changing. I felt things had gone topsy turvy and morale in the workplace was very low. Quality scientists who were often not good at writing grant proposals were missing out, while more entrepreneurial types were claiming success. The inevitable restructuring meant Jan's position would now be located in another state, so we decided to leave.

Jan got another job in a different area of the CSIRO,

but I wasn't sure that I wanted to do that. I began to think of myself as retired, but after spending several months working on the house, I found I had time on my hands. Jan persuaded me I needed to 'do something'. But what would this 'something' be?

When I was a kid most others wanted to be a pilot or an engine driver or a fireman. I wanted to be a taxi driver. I kept thinking about this and then I had an idea. My neighbour drove a hire car and I asked if I could do some part-time driving for him. I found I loved it and eventually when my neighbour's eyesight began to fail, he sold me his 'plate'. This seemed a good form of superannuation to me. I joined a cooperative of hire car drivers and joined the service. Retirement was put on the backburner.

DISASTER

I kept driving for almost another 20 years, but I didn't foresee that the NSW government would introduce legislation to deregulate the car hire industry just before the 2000 Olympics in Sydney, a move that had a devastating effect on my superannuation plans and that of other drivers. At one stroke my plates – I'd bought a second plate by this time – were made almost worthless. Of a Sunday evening Jan and I would be sending off 50 letters at a time. I even found myself marching with placards with hundreds of others outside Parliament House, something I'd never imagined I would do. I look differently now on people who do that because

I know what it is like to feel helpless and unable to right an injustice. It was a time that caused me a lot of heartache.

Not long after this I had a heart attack and then a bypass. It was totally unexpected, though I wasn't unaware of the possible connections with my earlier 'heartache'. To my surprise I found myself feeling a bit resentful that this had happened to me, but I think it was that reaction which spurred me on to recovery.

I went full steam ahead into rehabilitation and was lucky to have Jan's support in this – she was the only partner who joined in all the activities. We joined the 'Zipper and Stent' club at the Sydney Adventist Hospital in Wahroonga, a support group that encourages long-term maintenance rehabilitation for people who have had cardiac procedures. I was willing to do whatever I was told, and more, in order to fully recover. I wasn't going to give up on life.

I returned to work, but I was careful and more selective about the number of jobs I accepted. I found my colleagues' support in helping me out overwhelming, something that even now brings tears to my eyes. Luckily, at around this time the lobbying we'd done and our gradual increase in political nous began to bear fruit. The government offered us some fairly inadequate compensation, but the fact that they'd listened to the injustice of our situation and responded made all the difference to how we felt. The wounds began to heal and Jan and I prepared to retire for a second time.

THE KOKODA TRAIL

It was an annual custom for the Operation Open Heart organisation to take a team of cardiac experts to different third world countries where they supplied equipment and trained indigenous medicos. When they were in New Guinea some of the group visited Kokoda, and it was there that the idea for ex-cardiac patients to attempt the Kokoda Trail in the company of a medical team was born. I heard about this when Jan and I were at the Zipper and Stent Group working on my rehabilitation.

Bruce Haymen, formerly a CEO of the Australian Rugby Union, who'd had a quadruple bypass, and who is on various boards of directors and is president of the Zipper and Stent Group, wanted to make the dreams of the medical team into a reality. He decided to make a documentary to show the world what heart patients could do. Around $140 000 had to be raised to make the film, but he hoped that costs would be recovered through selling the film to television, and from selling the video and DVD.

I vividly recall the moment when I first heard of the request for volunteers to go to New Guinea. I looked at Jan and she looked at me. I knew I wanted to go and her face told me she would support me to the full. There were initially seven volunteers, but that dropped down to three – Bruce Haymen, aged 63, Jenny Dexter, a mother of four in her fifties, and myself also aged 63. We'd had 13 bypasses and a stent between us. I never considered not going.

I'd been keenly interested in the history of Kokoda when reading the divisional diaries and other books on the subject. I don't think enough is known about what happened in Kokoda. Everyone knows about Gallipoli and of course that is important, but Gallipoli was a British-led campaign and Australians were fighting as British subjects on foreign soil – and they were defeated. At Kokoda it was Australian troops on Australian soil (New Guinea was a protectorate), and it was a victory against incredible odds brought about by the spirit of a group of men who fought together for a cause they believed in.

I'd always been intrigued by the question as to how the 39th battalion – made up of 650 raggle-taggle members of the citizen military forces, or 'chockos' as they were affectionately nicknamed because it was thought they'd melt in the heat of battle – were able to stop the Japanese in their tracks. The Japanese, a seemingly invincible army of six to ten thousand, had steamrolled down the archipelago and were already bombing the north of Australia. Six months after the 39th battalion should have been relieved from their duties it was proving impossible to get replacement volunteers. What happened? All but two of the 39th regiment voluntarily returned – of the two who didn't return one had lost his leg and the other his arm.

I wanted to pay homage to these men and I also wanted to push myself a bit further – to live my life as fully as possible and to prove to myself that heart disease is not a death sentence. I also hoped the documentary would prove an inspiration to those who'd suffered the kind of setback my fellow travellers and I had survived.

I did a lot of training over the next seven months: carrying a 10 kilo sand bag in my backpack; working on a treadmill; trekking through the bush. It is said that the climbing involved is the equivalent of climbing Everest. It has also been rated as the third toughest trek in the world – the other two are at altitude. We three cardiac patients were to be accompanied by a medical team and 20 carriers. We knew if we were deep in the tropical jungle and another cardiac event occurred we would probably die. As one of the medical team says in the documentary, 'If something goes wrong there is not much I can do but sign the death warrant'.

There was an atmosphere of anticipation at Kokoda when we arrived, and camaraderie and good wishes from everyone. As we set off we knew there was a ten-day walk of 96 kilometres ahead of us in an unfamiliar, hot climate (the temperature was in the high 20s [°C] with about 90 per cent humidity – hydration was a constant problem) through rugged, difficult and uneven terrain. The jungle was thick and impenetrable, and we had to walk in single file. There was some beautiful tropical vegetation and exotic plants, although the native orchids were not in bloom. It was almost impossible to see the Birds of Paradise high in the canopy, but their calls were constantly around us.

In places the track was ankle deep in mud, and the footing was mostly uneven. It required a high degree of concentration just to place one foot in front of the other. I quickly learnt that the best way was to follow in the exact footsteps of Edwin, my young carrier. Our group of carriers spread out along the track for about 100 to 150 meters at any given time with the quicker walkers setting their own pace.

I found walking up the 'Golden Staircase' the most difficult part of the trek, and our doctors were quite concerned that the extra exertion was managed correctly. We encountered nine false crests; that is, the track would come to what appeared to be the top of the mountain, but then would turn and continue in another direction for perhaps another 100 or so meters, and then we would see the same depressing sight repeated – yet another 'crest' ahead.

It was harder than any of us imagined it would be. It was the most difficult thing I had ever attempted in my life. It really tested me. My greatest fear, of course, was that I'd let the others down and that was unthinkable. But I was very conscious that what I was going through was nothing compared to what the 39th battalion had suffered. I used to say to myself:

'John, you're a wimp. Think of what they went through – there is no one shooting at you.' In the end we three heart patients completed the walk successfully, and in fact were the only ones who didn't succumb to the various gastric ailments and other minor illnesses that others suffered. When we finally reached the end of the track I was truly elated. I felt forever connected to those who'd gone with me. It was an experience for which I'll be forever grateful.

Jan and I are now fully retired, you could say we're joined at the hip, and we divide our time between voluntary work with cardiac and cancer patients, health and exercise programs, travel plans within Australia, enjoying time with friends, and making our home close to being a self-sufficient haven. How are we finding it? It took Jan a bit longer to get used to it than I did. She puts this down to having been in a job that provided a structure she had to fit into, whereas I had been more able to create my own structure. At first she'd feel guilty all the time that she wasn't at a meeting or doing something someone had asked her to do. But fortunately that feeling is fading; in fact, it's almost gone right away now. I love saying 'yes' to things and now I have the time to do that. We think retirement is as good as winning the lottery.

Jean Guillermo: Blues sur Seine Festival organiser

I have not met Jean Guillermo in person. I heard of the interesting things he was doing in his retirement from a friend, Bill La Ganza, who lives in Paris. Bill helped me persuade Jean to be interviewed via email. Jean and I got to know each other a little this way and then I sent him a series of questions. Jean speaks excellent English, but he feels more at home writing in his native French. As a result, Bill kindly offered to translate his replies. When I read Jean's thoughtful responses to my questions I wanted others to hear what he had to say in his own words, or as close to as we could manage through a translation.

How and why did you decide to retire?
I was retired early at age 55. My employer wanted 95 per cent of employees 55 or over to leave with a special retirement plan guaranteeing 70 per cent of their income until they were old enough to benefit from retirement at the full rate. In my case, this would take five years, but for some others, who began to work late, this 'transitionary' period was to last for up to 12 years. It was not easy to make the decision to leave as I was doing a job I liked, that I was even passionate about. My position as an international consultant allowed me to meet people from markedly different businesses in many different countries.

My manager told me that I had been declared a

'strategic resource' for the company, which satisfied my ego and which was truly status enhancing at age 55. It meant that if I wanted to, I could stay in the company. I hesitated over several months, finding just as many reasons to leave and benefit from that exceptional offer, as to stay and continue in a job that I liked. Eventually, not having reached an agreement about future conditions, I decided to leave.

What sort of things did you think about and/or feel when you first retired?
The first thing was to get up a little later in the morning, as I no longer had one or one and a half hours' driving with the hassle of the traffic in order to get to work.

For two years I did a thousand little personal things: not being artistically inclined, I tried to find something that pleased me. I tried mosaics. Hard to find a course. Finally I found a municipal workshop in Paris, two half days per week. I, who am hyperactive, for whom things must move quickly, found slowness. A long time was necessary to shape pieces of stone or marble for tessellates, and then what humility to discover that the last blow of the hammer breaks the little piece of which I was so proud into smithereens or reduces it to powder. I discovered that I was not gifted, compared to the other students in the workshop, but I liked it. I was surprised to find that this craft, which was dirty (cement) and physical (preparing the tessellates), was valued, particularly by women.

At the same time, I attended as a student on Saturday mornings, 300 metres from my place, in a cultural and community centre, a Spanish course (which is where I met Bill). My naturally insatiable hunger led me to enrol as well in a Portuguese course, and Italian as well, and I must admit that if there were a common base between the three languages, the differences are such that I mixed everything up a bit. But that stems from the fact that I think of myself as a generalist, who tries a bit of everything, wanting to make the most of the diversity of the world in which we live.

In what ways did your life begin to change?
I needed in fact to be in contact with people as I had been in my professional life with my clients, my French colleagues and foreigners. I no doubt unconsciously looked for an activity that would allow me to network again with these contacts. This is why, during an office meeting of the association of the cultural centre where I was a committee member, I responded positively to the suggestion to create a blues festival, and I was in this way at the inception of, and am still fully engaged, nine years later in the Blues sur Seine festival, one of the largest examples of its kind in Europe, and which is widely recognised as being a highly original project in terms of its artistic, social and educative character.

I had no idea that, lacking sufficient numbers of personnel, particularly professional staff at the cultural centre, I would be the only one to look after the project, at least during the first year. A paid worker was taken on, as soon as I could gain the necessary funding, and today this festival is run not only by volunteers, but also by a team of three paid workers and an apprentice. It can't really be said that my life is less busy, as with the growing number of workers, I contributed to developing the festival in terms of the number of events, the number of towns involved, the length, the number of venues, the complexity of the administration, all of which has lead to an engagement in hours that totals more than I was formerly devoting to my professional life.

How did you feel about your new life?
I felt a sense of fulfilment. Another feeling is that I'm giving back something of what I have received. In the years just before my retirement, I think I probably told myself that it was high time to give back to the community in which I lived, to my town and to my region, a bit of the know-how that I had acquired during the first 55 years of my life. I also knew that people thought of me as creative, having ideas and as being 'contagious' for the people around me. To lend myself to a worthy cause and be its advocate, the one to spread the word, seemed to me to be heading in the right direction for the community, and at the same

time contributing to my own wellbeing and the self-assurance [in knowing] that I had become useful.

How do you mostly spend your time?
I work a lot from home (telephone and voicemail), but I regularly go to the office where the full-time staff of the association work, or to the evening meetings with other voluntary members of the association. I travel to meet elected local or regional members, public servants and businesses to try to convince them to take part in patronage or sponsoring. I frequently go to concerts; I go to other festivals two or three times a year for several days to find artists in France and Quebec; and I set up a twinning arrangement with a blues festival in Montreal. Then there are trips to Canada and the United States for meetings with other festival organisers and to promote French blues people.

All in all it's putting in the same amount of hours, or doubtless more hours, than I previously put into my professional life. I'm very motivated! This might explain my children's brewing criticism concerning my relative unavailability to look after and enjoy my grandchildren. At the same time, I tell myself that this rich life will no doubt allow me to have things to tell them in a few years.

Also my partner and I are aware of time's passing. She is very busy with her consultancy, but at the same time she is right to consider my engagement is no doubt excessive, as she is the witness that this volunteer work is mainly carried out at home. She respects my passion, understands that I need this escape, but at the same time would like me to ease off a little.

The striking difference between my former life as an executive in a multinational corporation and my present life as a volunteer completely engaged in a large project uniting local energies (associations, elected officials, teachers, colleagues, artists) is that now Saturdays and Sundays are no longer entirely devoted to my 'personal life'. During my professional life, I in effect 'protected' myself on the weekends. Now the telephone and especially voicemail invades my world and my hours of weekend time due to my using the excuse, for example, of the time difference with the United States or Canada. But, in fact, I'm responsible for this situation due to a lack of discipline!

Can you describe your sense of purpose?
The Blues sur Seine festival has a reputation for being a large enough initiative to create the following ties: intergenerational (we go as much into primary schools as into retirement homes); between communities (VIP evenings, corporate partner evenings, but also initiatives towards long-term prisoners, recovering accident victims in medical institutions, mentally handicapped children, the homeless and so on); and between people from different ethnic origins, immigrants, illegal immigrants, North African women and illiterate Africans.

This feeling of being in contact with the world at large is very rewarding, even if I tell myself that it is only a small stone brought to the whole global structure. Living happily together is important, particularly in a region like mine, which includes many immigrants in its population. It is my modest local contribution to the improvement of our world: 'think globally, act locally'.

Jane Sutherland: Artist

I met Jane Sutherland for the first time in 2006 at a friend's dinner party in New Haven, Connecticut. Jane and I were getting drinks from a table in the corner of a room decorated with pieces that caught the eye – a flying plaster angel; a collection of frogs; colourful tree of life sculptures from Mexico – an exotic background for a first meeting.

I explained that I was visiting from Australia and had just retired, and Jane said that she too was retired, having left her job seven years ago to concentrate full time on painting. I thought of this as a change of careers, but Jane rejected this idea: it was not how it seemed to her. I wanted to know more about why she saw herself as 're-tired'. She agreed to meet me a few days later in New Haven at Atticus, a cafe inside a bookshop, with just the right ambience for continuing our conversation. Her story unfolds.

FLOATING ANXIETIES

I spent about five years flirting with the idea of retirement before I made the decision to give up my position as a professor of fine arts at Fairfield University, Connecticut. I'd joined the staff there 28 years earlier after gaining my BA from Sarah Lawrence College, New York, and my Master of Fine Arts from Universidad de las Americas, Mexico DF, Mexico.

I had multiple anxieties about leaving the workforce. I was anxious about not contributing financially to my marriage as I'd always done and worried about my husband, Orin's, reaction to the idea of my retiring. I felt an obligation to my colleagues and students, and feared having to explain my decision to people, feeling afraid they'd think my reasons were not good enough. Nowadays people in academia don't generally leave the workplace until they're in their mid to late sixties – or even seventies. I was only 54. I had long thought how good it would be to paint full time, but lots of different things kept stopping me from telling anyone of my plans to retire, or taking any action towards that goal. What I later came to think of as 'floating anxieties' began to haunt me and act as a brake on what I dreamed of doing.

I also felt afraid I wouldn't be able to get my art out from the local to the national scene. There was a risk I would fail, and facing 'failure' was not something I felt good about. Having a senior tenured position at university was a financially secure option and provided me with a status that seemed foolish to give up. It is hard to explain, but somehow I felt that leaving my position would make me undesirable in many people's eyes, including my husband's, though I didn't face this for some time.

I spent a lot of energy getting nowhere and finally decided to turn to a therapist for advice. It was a good move though it took us some time to unravel my confused feelings. The therapist helped me recognise that the fear of not paying my way was a deep-seated concern for me, as I had always earned my living and saw this as an important part of my independence. I was worried about not making the same kind of financial contribution to our marriage [a second marriage] as I had from its beginning, and feared it would put us on an unequal footing. As it happened, my husband, when I finally talked to him about the idea, was very supportive, and that made a lot of difference to how I felt.

UNEMPLOYED AT LAST

In 1997, after five long years of prevarication, I said goodbye to my old life. I retired. Giving up tenure after 28 years of teaching made me feel as if I were returning to life as a civilian, as I had been in the academic community for most of my adult life. Retirement wasn't as traumatic as I'd thought it might be, although I often felt dismissed by members of the academic community, as if I were an outsider, and on social occasions I felt awkward and insignificant without my academic title. The 'retired' title seems to imply 'over the hill' to most people. I experienced a sense of loss but, perhaps, more as a loss of youth.

Being a full-time artist was what I wanted, but I wasn't looking for something as simple as 'fame' in planning to devote myself to my painting. It was more that I wanted a chance to make a new contribution to a field I care a great deal about. Teaching gave me this kind of satisfaction. In fact, I still teach at summer schools every year partly to revisit the feelings of engagement that it brings.

But as for being an artist being another career – no, that's not how I see it. I see an artist's life as a privileged life. The lack of affiliation with an organisation makes it seem self-serving and our culture may respect the idea of an artist, but it doesn't understand what an artist's life is about. Artists are not really valued by society; spending your day painting is not taken seriously in the same way as is working at a job. And it isn't regularly paid either. When I have an exhibition that I feel has expanded me, taken me further, then I feel some of the satisfaction I was hoping for, and if I sell some paintings as well that is an additional pleasure.

AN ARTIST'S LIFE

New opportunities in my field began to come my way. I was asked to write for a monthly art magazine from an editor who knew I had left teaching, and I still do that. I was accepted into a New York Gallery based on work I'd done previously, but it was too soon and I found myself painting previous themes. I was at a point where I should have been doing new things – well, I included some new themes, but none of them had a long life; they were more like branches on a tree, not the roots. I decided to leave the gallery and begin a new project. And yes, I went through all the old agonies but less so this time.

My days are structured – I know how many hours I need to put in at the studio and I try to work regular hours as if I have a real job. I think of my work as a real job. There are often real deadlines associated with exhibitions, catalogues, grant applications and so on. But I have elderly parents, a new grandchild and three children who live a good distance away whom I want to see as often as possible. I have to work hard to keep my own work going when other events come to the forefront of my life. It's a give and take that works as long as I stay on top of it all. Since I was a working mother all through my children's early years and since I am no longer 'working' it should all be possible.

A friend told me that in the first one or two years of retirement you are trying to prove that you are happy and that you've made the right choice, but you won't be really comfortable with yourself for some time. I thought in the first flush of retirement that I was really happy and that my friend was wrong. But then later I realised I had been deceiving myself. It takes time to find your centre or what your goal really is. I've always had clear ideas about other people, but cobwebs about myself. I'm more self confident now, more action oriented and able to 'seize the day'. I was holding myself back because I preferred to have the potential rather than to try and fail. I've realised now though that the potential is less fulfilling than the action. At first when I was asked 'What do you do?' I'd say 'I used to be a professor', but after I while I stopped referring to it – that is a sign that I've moved on.

FINDING A NEW DIRECTION

My new project is called Objects of Desire. I'm very excited about it because it is a new direction for me. I've chosen four female figures, rejected for various reasons, and I plan to use each of them for a series of paintings and drawings. There is Marie van Goethem, the 14-year-old ballet student and model, whose face was dubbed ugly and unattractive after Degas exhibited his *Little Dancer Aged Fourteen* in 1881; Tina Modotti, a photographer thought to have had an affair with Trotsky, who was expelled for her revolutionary activities in Mexico; Anna May Wong, a Chinese-American actress who was not allowed to kiss in films for cultural reasons and consequently was rejected for a part in Pearl Buck's film *Good Earth*; and Louise Brooks, a model for the flapper in silent movies in the 1920s, who was discovered and then rejected by Hollywood.

I've begun work on the Little Dancer – it has involved research and travelling to selected museum collections to see the wax original, the plaster cast and some of the bronzes cast after Degas' death. I've done a number of drawings now and I can see more clearly where I'm going. It is all beginning to come together.

Postscript

As you read the stories told here it is evident that personalities, personal histories and circumstances, and the conventions and values of the societies in which we live play a large part in shaping the life we choose for ourselves post-retirement. John Edward's commitment to his fellow car hire workers and their joint cause, his giving priority to not letting down his 'mates' on the Kokoda Trail journey, his wanting to do something that will help others, and his warm appreciation of his wife's selfless support suggest a person who would naturally be drawn to admire the achievements of the soldiers of the 39th battalion. He emulates their lives, albeit on a small scale in his own.

Jean Guillermo's generous-hearted response to questions from someone he has never met who lives on the other side of the world, in such a detailed and honest way, his tendency to try everything and want to be part of it all, his initiative and adventurous spirit, and his acceptance and faith in the goodness of people from wherever they hail suggest a person who will embrace a new project, lend it his energy and enthusiasm, and make it something through which he can begin to change the world in some small way for the better.

The multiple sensitivities displayed in Jane Sutherland's story – her punctilious sense of honour, her awareness of others' values and points of view and honesty about her own feelings, her lurking sense of humour, her belief in the power of art and creativity to transform lives, and her concern for things rejected suggest a person who will be unwavering in the use of her talents. She gives expression to a vision of those overlooked, or perhaps misinterpreted in this world, in a form that enables others to see them in a new way, and enjoy and appreciate the artistry that 'makes' them.

There was a special moment in my interview with Jane when we both recognised the link between her early reference to her fear of becoming 'undesirable' and the theme of her new project, 'Objects of Desire'. Neither of us said very much about it at the time, but the realisation of the connection shone there between us in a very satisfying way. Later Jane wrote to me about this moment:

I remember our mutual recognition of how my original fears of 'rejection' matched my description of how each of my figures had faced 'rejection' in their careers as well. The questions you asked and your listening style provoked me to do some listening to myself. You helped me make some connections that seemed so obvious. Well, for me it's often a case of 'dawn striking marble head' in terms of self-awareness!

Now that she is further on with her project, Jane says she is recognising other reasons for her being drawn to the figures she chose: 'Each of them represents qualities of human vanity, femininity, intelligence, wit and craft in different ways; they are proving endlessly intriguing.'

Similarly, after Bill La Ganza had translated Jean's comments, he said he'd enjoyed the experience because he'd 'learnt new things about an old friend'. He wondered if Jean, too, had seen his actions and reactions in a new light:

> I wonder if it was the first time that he had thought in so much depth about the whys and wherefores of his new direction, and the implications of this for his life and for those of others. Perhaps he had thought about one question or another from time to time, but it must have moved him to see the answers all together on the page, or, if not, to have given him a sense of the continuity of his professional life into retirement, and how his new activity has integrated into his social life and his own identity.

These responses are testimony to the importance of talking about and reflecting on what you are doing with your life in the various stages of your retirement. It is a topic of conversation that people usually treat humorously, but to take it more seriously can be illuminating.

Since these interviews took place, further evidence of the successes of the various projects has come to hand. The director of photography, Rod Turnbull, of the film *Kokoda with Heart*, received a Bronze Award from the Australian Cinematography Society. Sales of the film have now covered the costs of the enterprise. In addition, in 2007 the government provided a grant of $20 000 to allow the Zipper and Stent Group to place a copy of the DVD into every hospital Cardiac Unit throughout Australia.

Early in 2008, Jean Guillermo and his team received an international award for their work. Jean writes: 'Jay Sieleman (director of the Blues Foundation) came specially from Memphis to announce we have been given the international award for 'Keeping the Blues alive', an award based not on an evaluation of the past year, but on what we have achieved during the past nine years.'

Further confirmation of the success of the first stages of Jane's new project arrived in the post recently, in the form of a beautifully designed folding card announcing an exhibition of drawings and paintings, titled 'little dancer'. The full sequence of her paintings can be seen on her website at <http://www.janesutherland.com/index.html>.

The personal satisfaction of those whose work is discussed here is high and comes from their achieving what they set out to achieve after leaving their working lives behind. That they have achieved some measure of public success is an added bonus. Not everyone chooses to take on such challenges at this time: satisfaction and fulfilment are found in many different ways. Whatever the path you choose to follow, stories of those who set about realising particular ambitions can provide you with inspiration and encouragement.

Reflections

I've been trying, for nearly ten years, to
get a grip on this elusive thing

Franz T

When I began my research into the subject for this book I didn't expect to have a Eureka moment and suddenly understand what retirement was all about. And I haven't. I also wasn't expecting to unearth a formula from my interviews that people can apply to ensure happiness or satisfaction in retirement. And, as expected, I didn't unearth any failsafe solutions. This is not to say that people don't have many suggestions that represent good advice for most people – do something for others and for yourself every day; keep physically and mentally fit or occupied; let go of the past and create a new identity for yourself; don't just fill in the time – find a meaningful direction; organise an income that will be sufficient ('how?' 'If only I could', I hear you say) and so on. But advice, however useful, doesn't necessarily deepen your understanding of how you and retirement are going to get along. Many people distrust advice or think it won't apply to their particular case. I recall Arthur Smith, the English comedian of *Grumpy Old Men* fame, making that clear. 'It's all very well about that "carpe diem" stuff. I don't want people telling me to seize the day and to live in the now. Why not let the day have a little run by itself ...'

You can, however, learn much about the nature of the experience of retirement in the twenty-first century from listening to, and talking with, others. And when you step back to reflect on the subject of the new retirement, you begin to get beneath the surface gloss that is a part of retirement solutions advertising, media representations and even folk wisdom. There are many observations that can be made, but I shall confine myself to making some general comments that strike me as being worthy of further consideration before presenting some more personal reflections.

Before I move on to this, however, I want to acknowledge that I realise I've mainly been writing about people who live in affluent societies where there are many choices and possibilities available. I am painfully aware that this isn't true for many of the world's peoples, particularly those living in impoverished countries where survival is a miracle and a hope, but by no means a certainty. At the same time life doesn't discriminate between the peoples of the world when tragedies and illnesses occur. In the later years of life you probably become more aware of its darker side, and recognise that unpredictable events, whether for good or ill, can occur at any time. Feste's words in *Twelfth Night*, 'What's to come is still unsure', are true for all of us, all of the time.

~

Retirement is a time of uncertainty, but it's also a time of vulnerability. You become exposed to the idea that you are only a meaningful member of human society if you are engaged in some recognised occupation. There is a common assumption that retired people have little or nothing to do except to fill in their time. While comments implying this are usually offered in an affable, good-humoured way, they perpetuate a concept of retirement as a demeaning, relatively futile time in your life. Mark Haddon, in his novel, *A Spot of Bother* (Jonathan Cape, 2006, pp. 49–50 Copyright © Mark Haddon 2006), presents an exchange between two of his characters, George, the husband of Jean, and David, her lover, that comically illustrates their uneasy awareness about the way society positions you once you are retired:

> 'Keeping busy?' asked George.
> 'David laughed. 'I thought the point of retiring was that we no longer had to be busy.'
> George laughed. 'I guess so.'

We don't have very good ways of dealing with the thought that valuable and interesting lives can be lived outside the boundaries of 'useful' occupations. Oscar Wilde, the Irish playwright, undermined nineteenth-century utilitarian ideals as vigorously as he challenged their conceptions of sexual stereotypes. As he says, in 'The Critic as Artist': 'The sure way of knowing nothing about life is to try to make oneself useful'.

A friend visiting from London passed on to me an idea that came to her from a friend of hers who had felt deeply insulted by her dinner companion (at a college high table, no less), turning his back very quickly after she'd answered his 'What do you do?' question, with the reply that she was 'at home'. Being asked what you do can be confronting, particularly if you are not in the workforce, and to say you are 'at home' or 'retired' can seem to suggest some kind of inadequacy on your part. Her friend decided it would be much more inviting and conversationally productive to ask others what interests them, a course she now follows with rewarding results.

Important phases of life, or 'Passages' as Gail Sheehy nicely describes them, usually involve the idea of a steep learning curve for those venturing into them. Somehow, ideas about retirement in the public domain tend not to be associated with expectations of this kind. There is a general consensus that, once you get there, you are on your own and your learning curves are over: you should relax and have a good time. Yet retirement is a beginning, as well as an ending, and as with any major new experience there is much to learn. You have to learn the ropes of your unfamiliar situation; understand what 'a good time' involves for someone of your personality, talent and skills; find a path through the maze of possibilities before you; and prepare for the different phases that lie ahead. Retirement is a learning experience.

You have to learn how to let go of your past. The symbols of your past life – your desk, your tools of trade, your office phone or mailbox – no longer belong to you. This is a difficult realisation, even a shock. When the last trappings of your connections with the workplace are dismantled it can make you feel as if you don't exist. This happens to everyone, whatever their status. After resigning from the position of prime minister of England, Harold Macmillan, at the time in his hospital bed, was interrupted by a post office engineer who came to his bedside to remove his red phone, his personal hotline to government. The irritating explanation, 'You're not prime minister any more, you know', was, understandably, not very well received.

Letting go of the work ethic of a lifetime is another aspect about which there is very little advice or help available. Letting go, it is said, allows you to better see new opportunities that are there for the taking. Learning to deal with feelings of loss and change, and of being discarded, is something most people do alone, but it is helpful to realise that talking about how you feel is a legitimate stage in the process of adjusting, and not a sign of failure, or of not coping.

How to establish a new or different sense of identity for yourself, one that is not tied to the workplace, but with which you feel comfortable, is something else you may have to learn to do as you set about creating yourself in retirement. Most people need to feel they are leading purposeful lives. Some people, of course, feel they've earned the right to do as they please and don't feel any need to define themselves differently, or even at all. Others have occupations that make relatively easy the transition from a previous working identity to a different version of that identity – academics, for example, become writers or continue with their research – and they continue to see themselves in much the same way as they have always done.

Those in occupations that don't allow such ready transitions can have more difficulty finding a sense of purpose or a satisfying role. I talked with some people who fear, along with Hamlet, that if they don't take action soon then their energy, skills and capabilities might 'fust in us unused'. It is always easier not to make changes, particularly when life is pretty good anyway, and you can't put your finger on what it is you'd really like to do. Sometimes people who aren't sure what they'd like to do are out of the habit of listening with their inner ear to their own needs and desires, or as someone wrote to me in a moment of despair about some of her retired friends: 'They don't know what they really want, or what there is to want'.

It seems to be a fact of human nature that people are aware that in historical terms things are always changing, but in their own case they manage to envisage a future where things stay exactly the same. People often plan their retirement imagining that current choices will be their only choices. This is in spite of the fact that the radical worldwide shift in demographics taking place now indicates our immediate futures will involve tidal waves of economic, social and cultural change.

Moving into a retirement village, once a sentence to days of relative inactivity and confinement, is likely to be quite a new kind of experience in the near future. Trends in this increasing market include the grouping of people with similar interests together, such as in Beth Gornick's brainchild, the 'House of Elder Artists' in New York, or creating communities founded on spiritual principles that mix a proportion of younger residents in with more elderly people, as happens in some places in Spain. Retirement villages, more generally, are said to be undergoing a 'rethink', providing golf courses, gyms, swimming pools and other facilities for a range of physical activities, and offering extensive social programs. As Kathy Buchanan suggests in her comments about the A-List status retirement villages are acquiring, 'a visit to Gran is looking pretty good right now', and is only likely to improve (*Sunday Telegraph Magazine*, Sydney, 27 January 2008).

It is not yet clear how future generations will view the role of work in their lives, but it is clear that notions of what it means to 'work' and to be 'retired' are no longer always thought of as mutually exclusive, and that the relationship between them will continue to change. New financial options, often referred to as 'transition to retirement strategies', that support phasing out of your working life gradually, or at a pace to suit, are now on the market. Some companies, too, are beginning to recognise that hiring older workers on a part-time basis, possibly after retraining, may make good business sense. Trends of this kind will make working more selectively for shorter periods, or retraining to take up a different kind of work for limited hours, a more viable option for many.

People's interest in returning to some kind of 'work' after officially retiring is not necessarily financially motivated, but rather connected with wanting to continue to make a contribution, to have a purpose, and to feel you are not yet socially redundant. Surveys taken in 2008 in different places around the world confirm that people are doing more in retirement than they have ever done before. They want 'to get up and go', to 'rediscover' or 'reinvent' themselves, rather than to sit idly at home (except, perhaps, for Arthur Smith). People are returning to work part time, taking up demanding projects, and engaging in extensive voluntary, unpaid work, yet they think of themselves as being retired. It is difficult to predict the next stage of this process, but it seems likely that distinctions between work and retirement will continue to blur at the edges.

~

I am more at home with retirement now that I have spent almost two years 'in the saddle'. At the same time, although I have learned a great deal on the subject, I regard my thoughts as being very much a work in progress. Many of these thoughts are included in an incidental way in earlier chapters, but if I were to draw together those I've found most helpful, I'd suggest the following:

- You can try to imagine what retirement will be like for you, but it is hard to anticipate the actual nature of the experience. You prepare financially, of course, but it is difficult to prepare emotionally, or in terms of what you'll be doing. I found it useful to begin work on what I planned to do before I actually left work. In that way, at least, I was able to test out whether my plans were ill chosen, or not what I wanted to do after all.
- You think that by the time you retire you know all there is to know about yourself. But you probably don't. I've learned a great deal in these last two years, particularly about my strengths and weaknesses. It is because there is time to think more about your reactions to things; time to experiment with things you haven't tried before; and you are the one

making the decisions about what you'll be doing and when you'll do it.

- Work provides you with a powerful routine or structure, but when you are without this you need to create your own structure – a heady responsibility! It isn't easy to get the rhythm and the balance right and it can take a considerable time before you feel you come near to doing so. Maybe you never really do get it quite right ...

- Retirement has many different phases and you can't live them all at once. It is easy to expect too much of yourself, particularly in the early stages. On the other hand there is the danger of drifting for so long that you lose direction altogether.

- It is all too easy to waste time and energy on feeling guilty. So you haven't begun that voluntary work you planned to do; you haven't started sorting out your old tax files or the family history. There is no point in beating yourself over the head with recriminations when deep down you know you are not going to do these things just now.

- Fear can drive the decisions you make – fear that if you say 'no' to a job, a lunch or an opportunity, there will never be an offer like it again, and you'll fade in people's minds as a person of worth. These are often unnecessary fears. You don't want to throw caution to the winds, but you don't want to fill your time with things you really don't want to do.

- Retirement is an adventurous time, not necessarily an adventure of the thrill a minute or the climbing Everest kind, but in the sense that you are centre stage with control of the action, and you don't quite know what will happen next in this intriguing stage of your life.

- It seems to me that when you are retired you face life more simply and directly than at any other time. You don't want to be intimidated by other people's values, achievements or lifestyles, but talking about the real issues with them can be illuminating as well as comforting, and helps to establish your own perspective.

Trying to understand retirement is a bit like trying to understand life. Not at all easy. I am beginning to come to terms with what it means, although I do have a certain fellow feeling with Franz T's comments about its elusive nature. What I'm finding particularly hard at present is to 'get the rhythm right'. When I become absorbed in something it devours all my time and energies. I neglect, even forget about, other things that I know I should be, or would like to be doing, and I fail to leave any time or space for doing nothing much at all.

Now that I've almost finished working on this book, I worry about what life will be like without it. Will I get withdrawal symptoms? Will I start another project and lose the will to finish it? Will I feel like a beached whale and not know what to do with myself? I realise these are the 'normal' anxieties that plague making the transition from one phase to another, but that doesn't stop me worrying about possibilities. A report I came across recently found that the average Brit spends five years, two months of their life worrying. Five years, two months! Don't ask me how they measured this, but I felt better immediately on reading it. I couldn't possibly be that bad, could I?

I'm also taking precautions against the beached whale syndrome. I'm about to start a class in botanical drawing, something I've always wanted to do, and I'm already in conversation with my grandchildren over our third book in a series about a Rainbow Dragon that we're writing and illustrating together. It is called *The Dragon Lover*.

Now that I'm poised here, in the very last paragraph of my book, I have a strong sense of loss washing over me, conscious of leaving behind a project that closely connected me with people who allowed me into their lives. But it is time to leave this behind and turn to something different. And, when some more time has passed, I know there will be new feelings of excitement and anticipation for what lies ahead.